£1.95

A taste of
the North East

First published 2005
by Newcastle Chronicle & Journal Ltd
Groat Market,
Newcastle Upon Tyne, NE1 1ED
ISBN 9511-095-7-X

Editors: Kathryn Armstrong, Huw Lewis
Design Editor: Ian Guy
Sales Manager: Mark Anderson

Tableware supplied by Crosbys, Newcastle
www.crosbys.co.uk

Printed by The Journal Print Company

A taste of
the North East

Photography by Nicky Rogerson & Kevin Gibson

CONTENTS

INTRODUCTION

While we've been working on this tasty book one phrase has been repeated time and time again. Local produce.

It seems there has been a real about turn from chefs and restaurants away from 'show-off' food and back to basics.

Not least because that's what customers are demanding too.

We care like never before about the origin of our food and are now prepared to stand proud and demand that we eat locally sourced food that hasn't been on a round-the-world journey before it gets to our plate.

The chefs in this, the second volume of A Taste of the North East , are all dedicated to serving the best produce they can get their hands on - whether it's Craster crab, Northumberland lamb or organic herbs from County Durham.

They're positively rejoicing that their gospel of good food is being adopted by 'at home' chefs too and we're all lucky that the growing number of farmers' markets, farm shops and organic producers is helping us get a taste of what 'real food' is all about.

Within our pages you're going to find some stunning recipes. Some made for formal entertaining, some for rustic, relaxed suppers, some to challenge but all to savour and swoon over.

The recipes come from the kitchens of some of the North East's best -loved and industry-acclaimed restaurants and we've also included a directory of local suppliers so you can always get you hands on the freshest, finest ingredients.

So, time to get that apron on, knife out and wine open.

Kathryn Armstrong

Editor, Exclusive Magazine

AGE BAR

AGE BAR

Age bar and Kitchen in Claypath, Durham City, should be pre-fixed with the word Any. That's the concept behind the place - anyone, any age, could love it. Terry and Michelle Breen do. This is the first year in their own restaurant and they're loving it. Terry has been in the restaurant trade much of his life but Michelle has given up teaching to live their dream.

Age is a stunning building in one of Durham's oldest streets. A contemporary feel pays homage to the past as the decor combines original, characterful oak beams with today's craftsmanship in wood. The effect is charming and welcoming – just like Terry and Michelle.

I work with Terry devising our menu. It is simple, but like an increasing number of restaurants, concentrates on quality ingredients rather than flamboyant descriptions. It's likely your rack of lamb has been brought up near the restaurant itself, such is the desire for local to mean local. Terry trots down to the indoor market to source local cheeses and while there can find the freshest fish that day... to appear on his menu later.

Once your food arrives it has its quirkiness too – mussels come in a huge galvanised bucket with chips served in another just a bit smaller.

For us it's about quality but fun and a touch of theatre too – a Chateaubriand fillet steak will arrive at your table with a flourish, to be mouth-wateringly carved before your very eyes.

Stephen McNally, head chef

Duck bresola

Serves 4

INGREDIENTS

1 duck breast, skin, fat and sinew removed

MARINADE:
1 tsp sea salt
$^1/_2$ tsp black peppercorns
$^1/_2$ tsp ground coriander
6 cardomon pods
4 star anise
juice and zest of 1 unwaxed orange and 1 unwaxed lemon
2 tbs olive oil

METHOD

To prepare, grind the dry marinade ingredients together then add lemon, orange and olive oil and mix together. Coat the duck in the marinade and refrigerate. After 24 hours turn the duck and leave for another 24 hours. Rinse the marinade off the duck then pat the meat dry and wrap in muslin or a clean linen tea-towel then refrigerate for 48 hours. Before serving, remove the muslin/cloth and freeze for 10-15 minutes for slicing. Then slice as thinly as possible. Serve with a crisp salad of chopped spring onion, bean sprouts and cucumber, drizzled with honey and sesame oil.

Monkfish wrapped in Parma ham with ratatouille vegtables

Serves 4

INGREDIENTS

4 150g pieces of monkfish

8 slices of Parma ham

butter for frying

RATATOUILLE:

fresh thyme stalks

1 shallot, finely diced

1 red pepper, finely diced

1 yellow pepper, finely diced

$1/2$ courgette, finely diced

$1/2$ aubergine, finely diced

100ml vegetable stock

METHOD

For the fish, fillet and skin the monkfish to remove all the sinew – a fishmonger will be able to cut portions of fish to size for you. Wrap the monkfish pieces in the Parma ham then tightly wrap the parcels in cling film and place in the fridge for an hour. Heat a non-stick pan and add a knob of butter. Remove the fish from the fridge and take off the cling film. Add the fish to the pan and seal on each side for about a minute. Season with salt and freshly ground black pepper. Bake the fish in a hot oven for about eight minutes. Once cooked, allow to rest for a couple of minutes before slicing and arranging on the ratatouille vegetables.

For the ratatouille, sweat the onion in a little butter for two minutes. Add the aubergine and peppers and cook for a further two minutes, then add the courgette and cook for two minutes more. Add the thyme and vegetable stock and cook for approximately five minutes. Remove the thyme stalks then season with salt and pepper.

* To make a chive oil for drizzling around the finished dish, take a small bunch of chives and blanch them in boiling water for 15 seconds, refresh in cold water immediately and pat dry. Blend the chives with 200ml of olive oil and pass through a fine sieve.

AGE BAR

Chocolate mocha pots with biscotti di prato

Serves 6

INGREDIENTS

CHOCOLATE POTS:

$^1/_2$ pint double cream

175g chocolate (plain) broken into pieces

6 egg yolks

1 double espresso coffee

75g butter melted

3 tbs brandy

BISCOTTI DI PRATO:

(Makes about 24 biscuits)

50g almonds (whole)

50g pistachios (whole)

450g self-raising flour

300g sugar

100g butter

4 eggs

Zest of one orange

METHOD

For the chocolate pots, warm the cream in a pan on the stove, but do not allow to boil. Whisk in the coffee, egg yolks and brandy. Cool slightly then add melted butter. Pour into espresso cups for serving then chill. Decorate with cocoa powder when chilled.

For the biscuits, mix together the flour, butter, sugar and orange zest. Add the nuts and eggs and mix to a paste. Roll out into a log. Bake in a hot oven for 15-20 minutes and allow to cool. Slice thinly into discs and bake them flat on a tray in the oven for a further ten minutes.

AGE BAR & KITCHEN

72 Claypath, Durham, DH1 1QT
Tel: 0191 375 7750, www.agebarandkitchen.co.uk

BALTIC

BALTIC

I started my career as a chef at McCoys at the Tontine, before working in Canada, the Caribbean, and many other places. I returned to the UK to become head chef at the Tontine, eventually going into business with the McCoy brothers in 1990. As well as being chef proprietor of McCoys at Baltic, I also design menus for GNER first class food and have a successful consultancy business.

Simon Wood is now head chef at McCoys at Baltic, having spent several years working in Sydney, Australia. He works very closely with me to design menus that are at the cutting edge of contemporary modern cuisine in the North East. We are unapologetic in trying out new things on the menus, believing that the fine dining experience should be memorable, that food should be challenging, and that restaurants in the North East should be comparable with the world's top restaurants.

Marcus Bennett, chef proprietor, McCoys at BALTIC
Simon Wood, head chef, McCoys at BALTIC

BALTIC

Assiette of foie gras. Foie gras mousse, foie gras brulee and seared foie gras with brioche and onion marmalade, served with apple chutney, grapes and a Madeira sauce

Serves 4

INGREDIENTS

FOIE GRAS MOUSSE:

227g foie gras
450g duck liver
1 onion finely diced
2 cloves of garlic
100ml brandy and 100ml port

FOIE GRAS BRULEE:

4 egg yolks
$1/2$ pint cream
100g foie gras softened
1 tsp truffle oil
salt and pepper

METHOD

For the foie gras mousse, cook the onions and garlic in a little butter until soft. Add the duck liver and foie gras and cook for a further 10 minutes until the livers are browned on all sides but still pink in the middle. Reduce the brandy and port by half and add to the livers. Liquidise the mixture and season with salt and pepper. For the foie gras brulee, whisk the egg yolk and cream together and place in a bowl over a pan of simmering water, whisking the mixture until it coats the back of a spoon. Liquidise the foie gras and truffle oil together and add to the brulee mix. Finally, season and with salt and pepper and pour into shot glasses to set. For the seared foie gras with brioche and onion marmalade, sear four 30g pieces of foie gras in a pan. For the onion confit place 6 onions, peeled and finely sliced, 25g unsalted butter, juice of 1 lemon, 2 tsp salt, 2 tsp pepper in a pan and cook over a low heat covered for 30 minutes, stirring occasionally until it looks like a brown stew. Cut the brioche into a small circle and toast it. Put some of the onion marmalade and the seared foie gras on top of the brioche. For the madeira sauce, put 2 pints of chicken stock in a pan and reduce by half. Add $1/2$ pint of Madeira, 1 tsp of sugar and $1/2$ tsp salt, and simmer for two minutes. To serve, quenelle the foie gras mousse. Serve the foie gras brulee in a shot glass. Line up all the elements on a long plate. Garnish with diced apple and crushed ginger biscuit. Pour the sauce around the plate to flavour and decorate, add the grapes.

BALTIC

The Rooftop Restaurant, South Shore Road, Gateshead
Tel: 0191 440 4949

BALTIC

Rack of lamb with rhubarb chutney, roasted rhubarb and white bean puree

Serves 4

INGREDIENTS

4 individual 1-pin racks of lamb

CONFIT OF LAMB SHOULDER:

1 shoulder of lamb, salted

4 pints of duck fat, melted in a large metal roasting tin

2 heads of garlic

2 sprigs of thyme

RHUBARB CHUTNEY:

450g rhubarb

1 onion finely diced

100g sugar

50ml red wine vinegar

25ml red wine

PICKLED RHUBARB:

9 batons of rhubarb

$^1/_4$ pint of red wine vinegar

$^1/_4$ pint of grenadine

METHOD

For the lamb, seal the rack in a frying pan until browned on all sides. Place in the oven at 220C for ten minutes, remove and leave to rest for five minutes. Slice off either end to expose the meat. **For the confit,** wash the salt off the lamb shoulder and place it in the duck fat with the garlic and thyme. Cover the tin in foil and cook at 150C for four hours. Remove the lamb from the fat and drain it. Roll in cling film and mould into a sausage shape. **To make white bean puree,** bring 100ml of cream to the boil with two garlic cloves and 250g of white beans and simmer for ten minutes. Liquidise, season and add 1tsp of truffle oil. **For the chutney,** put the sugar, red wine vinegar and red wine in a pan and bring to the boil. Add the onion and simmer for ten minutes. Add the rhubarb and simmer over a low heat for 25 minutes. **To make pickled rhubarb,** bring the red wine vinegar and grenadine to the boil in a pan. Pour over the rhubarb in a dish and leave to marinate for six hours. **Make a mint and spinach puree** by softening a shallot in a pan with 1tsp of red wine vinegar. Put this in a blender with $^1/_2$lb of picked, washed spinach, 24 blanched mint leaves and 1tsp of Dijon mustard. blend until a smooth puree is made. Season with salt and pepper. **Make a port jus** by reducing two pints of chicken stock by half, adding half a pint of port and simmering for two minutes. **To serve,** place the rack of lamb on the plate. Quenelle the rhubarb chutney. Place the confit lamb on plate, then white bean puree on top, before adding a baton of pickled rhubarb. Quenelle the mint and spinach puree and place it next to the confit lamb. Decorate the plate with port sauce.

BALTIC

The Rooftop Restaurant, South Shore Road, Gateshead
Tel: 0191 440 4949

BALTIC

Dark chocolate mousse with pistachio ice cream, chocolate caramel, lime jelly and chocolate paint

Serves 4

INGREDIENTS

CHOCOLATE MOUSSE BASE:

75g of white chocolate

2 tbs of double cream

1 tsp of liquid glucose

3oz of paillette feuilleline paste

1 tbsp of praline paste

CHOCOLATE MOUSSE:

300g dark chocolate

4 egg yolks

125g caster sugar

90ml of cold water

300ml of double cream

100ml milk

LIME JELLY:

$1/4$ pint of lime juice

$1/4$ vanilla pod, split, seeds removed

3 sheets gelatine

CHOCOLATE SAUCE:

200g chocolate

160ml milk

3 tbs cream

30g sugar

30g butter

Pistachio ice cream:

lt milk

$1/2$ lt cream

12 egg yolks

100g sugar

1 tbs pistachio paste

METHOD

For the base, melt the chocolate with the cream, then stir in the glucose and the praline paste and finally fold in the paillette feuilleline. Press the mixture into 2 inch diameter moulds and leave to set in the fridge. **For the mousse,** melt the dark chocolate and leave to cool at room temperature. Whisk the egg yolks and caster sugar in a bowl over simmering water until you achieve a thick golden foam, then fold in the melted chocolate and chill in the fridge. Whip the cream and the milk together until it forms soft peaks, then fold the cream into the chocolate mixture. Pour into the moulds and leave to set in the fridge. **For the lime jelly,** soak the gelatin to soften. Bring lime juice and vanilla to the boil and add the gelatine to the mix. Stir until dissolved and pour into moulds, leaving to set. **For the chocolate sauce,** melt the chocolate over a low heat in a bowl over water. Warm the milk and cream with the sugar until it is dissolved and add to the chocolate. Whisk in the butter until smooth. **For the ice cream,** boil the cream and milk. Whisk the egg yolks with the sugar until pale and creamy. Whisk in the milk and cream over a low heat until it coats the back of a spoon. Add the pistachio paste and churn in an ice cream machine, or freeze for 20minutes, then churn again, repeating this until frozen. **To serve,** paint the chocolate sauce down the middle of the plate. Slice the mousse in half and place on one side of the line. Place the lime jelly and pistachio ice cream on the other side and sprinkle with pistachio nuts.

BALTIC

The Rooftop Restaurant, South Shore Road, Gateshead
Tel: 0191 440 4949

BARN MOVING ON!

BARN MOVING ON!

My cooking is global and I love to produce food from around the world in interesting and innovative combinations; dishes that people wouldn't normally be able to find in Newcastle. My favourite dishes are the more creative ones, something I learnt when I worked for almost a year in Perth, Australia. When I first arrived in Perth, the range of food the chefs were producing just blew me away because their international influences were so vast. I loved working there, and when I came back to the North East I was keen to try the dishes I had created in Australia on the local clientele.

I left Australia six years ago and joined Mark Lagun at Barn Again in Newcastle, and have enjoyed three great years at the Biscuit Factory. 2006 is going to be an exciting time for us as we move out of the Biscuit Factory to two fantastic new venues in Jesmond and Bath Lane, Newcastle. The Jesmond restaurant "Barn Roaming Again" will allow us to continue the inventive fusion cooking we are famous for and "Barn and Gone to Vietnam", as the name suggests, will be a new adventure in Eastern cooking. Our brigade of nine chefs will move with us, with me working between the two restaurants. We hope these smaller venues will allow us to offer a more intimate dining experience, and develop further the customer-focused ethos the Barn has always been about.

Brian James, head chef

BARN MOVING ON!

Seared scallops with red braised belly pork, chilli lime caramel and oyster shooter

Serves 4

INGREDIENTS

8 scallops

700g piece of skinless, boneless belly pork

4 fresh, shelled oysters in 4 shooter glasses with a chilled liquor of sake, mirin and wasabi

CHILLI LIME CARAMEL:

200g grated palm sugar

200ml water

1 red chilli, sliced

1 green chilli, sliced

zest and juice of one lime

RED BRAISING LIQUOR:

2 lt water

300ml Shaohsing rice wine

200g yellow rock sugar

300ml dark soy sauce

100ml light soy sauce

3 star anise

1 cinnamon stick

1 10cm ginger root, peeled and sliced

3 peeled garlic cloves

3 spring onions

300ml orange juice

3 red chillies, split

METHOD

For the liquor, place all ingredients in a large pan and bring to a boil and simmer for 30 minutes. Remove from heat and cool, then strain through a fine sieve and discard solids. Bring liquid back to the boil in a large saucepan then add pork belly and simmer gently for up to two hours or until tender. Weigh down with a plate if necessary to keep submerged in liquor. Remove pork and place between two baking trays with some heavy weights on top and press until cool then refrigerate. After about five hours, remove and cut into 12 3cm cubes. For the chilli lime caramel dissolve palm sugar in water on a low heat. Bring to a boil. Simmer until reduced to about 100ml or until golden brown. Remove from heat, cool slightly and stir in chillies, zest and juice of lime. To prepare, heat a heavy-based frying pan with a little oil on a high heat and sear seasoned scallops on both sides for 1-2 minutes or until golden brown. Deep fry belly pork at 180C until crisp and then season with salt. To serve, place scallops and pork on a long, narrow plate with oyster shooter at one end. Drizzle scallops and pork with chilli lime caramel.

* Red braising stock can be used again for the same meat, just pass through a fine sieve, skim off fat and re-boil for six minutes. Cool quickly by adding a little ice and then freeze.

BARN MOVING ON!

The Biscuit Factory, Shieldfield, Newcastle
Tel: 0191 230 3338

BARN MOVING ON!

Tataki of tuna with shicuimi-togarashi, soba noodle salad and wasabi mayonnaise

Serves 4

INGREDIENTS

4 pieces 180g yellowfin tuna

shicuimi-togarashi (Japanese seven-spice powder, available from Asian supermarkets)

200g cooked soba noodles

1 long, red chilli, finely sliced

3 spring onions, finely sliced at an angle

1 ruby grapefruit, segmented

coriander leaves

nori seaweed

WASABI MAYONNAISE:

1 43g tube wasabi paste

5 tsp rice vinegar

50g pasturised egg yolks

330ml peanut oil

5 tsp Kikkoman soy sauce

fish sauce

METHOD

To prepare, place wasabi, egg yolks and rice vinegar in a food processor with motor running and slowly drizzle oil until a thick mayonnaise is formed then add soy sauce and process again until well incorporated. Check seasoning and refrigerate. Coat tuna in a light covering of the togarashi spice and wrap in clingfilm and tighten at both ends to form a cylinder shape, refrigerate for two hours.

To serve, remove tuna from the fridge and unwrap. Season with salt and sear in a hot, heavy-based frying pan coated with a little peanut oil until cooked on the outside but still pink in the middle. Remove from pan and cool slightly. Mix all the salad ingredients together in a large bowl and add a splash of lime juice, fish sauce and peanut oil. Divide between four plates and top with seaweed. Slice tuna into five or six slices and arrange on a plate with wasabi mayonnaise and extra togarashi for seasoning.

BARN MOVING ON!

Chocolate and hazelnut caramel tart

Serves 12

INGREDIENTS

SWEET PASTRY:

240g plain flour

90g icing sugar

100g unsalted butter, chopped

25g cocoa powder

2 eggs

FILLING:

200g soft dark brown sugar

100g butter, chopped

180ml double cream

300g skinless hazelnuts

500g dark chocolate, 53% cocoa solids

370ml whipping cream

METHOD

For pastry, sift flour, icing sugar and cocoa powder into a large mixing bowl. Add butter and work into a fine crumb. Add eggs and mix until pastry comes together. Wrap in clingfilm and refrigerate for 20-30 minutes. Roll out to cover a 10-inch wide 1$^1/_2$-inch deep tart ring and blind bake at 180C for 12 minutes, then cool.

For filling, place hazelnuts in a food processor and process until a coarse texture is achieved. Combine sugar, double cream and butter in a large saucepan and bring to the boil, slowly stirring until the sugar and butter melt. Continue to cook on a low heat for six minutes then stir in hazelnuts and cook for a further three minutes or until thickened. Pour into the tart case and spread evenly then refrigerate for an hour. For topping, bring whipping cream to boil, remove from heat and stir in chocolate until smooth and shiny then pour into tart case and refrigerate until set. Cut into 12 pieces and serve with ice-cream – we use white chocolate and cookie flavour.

BARN MOVING ON!

The Biscuit Factory, Shieldfield, Newcastle
Tel: 0191 230 3338

THE BLACK DOOR

BLACK DOOR

It's been a dream of mine for many years to own and run a restaurant, but I never quite expected it to be so far away from my Devonian roots. But since arriving in the North East in 1991 I've fallen in love with the place.

It's been a long journey through many a kitchen to get here – from the Grosvenor House on Park Lane, where I worked for nearly four years to the kitchen of Paul Gaylor at the Halkin Hotel then, having met my wife Debbie, back to her home town of Newcastle where I worked for Terry Laybourne's 21 Queen Street for ten years.

It was here particularly that my thoughts and perceptions of food were moulded, and a lot of this experience has been put into place at the Black Door.

It's not only the food that has to be right, but everything, from the welcome at the door to pre-dinner drinks and the service that we provide. The whole package must be perfect.

We source as many local products as we can – both food and drink – because increasingly that is what the customer demands.

We've just picked up an award from the Harden's Guide in conjuction with Remy Martin, affirmation that Black Door is getting it right, and we will strive to keep it so.

David Kennedy, head chef

BLACK DOOR

Tranche of foie gras, puy lentils, giroles and Maderia sauce

Serves 4

INGREDIENTS

500g foie gras – 125g per portion

300g puy lentils-soaked in water, then cooked for 15mins

300g giroles mushrooms. cleaned then cooked in a little butter

500g chicken wings, chopped

400ml Maderia

50ml sherry vinegar

200g shallots, finely chopped

100g button mushrooms, finely sliced

3 cloves of garlic, finely sliced

2lts veal/brown chicken stock

20g butter

METHOD

To prepare, brown the chicken bones, and add the shallots, mushrooms and garlic. Caramelise these to give maximum flavour. Add the vinegar, reduce until dry, add Maderia, reduce by half, add the stock and reduce by two-thirds. In a very hot pan, season then sear the foie gras on both sides; this will take about two minutes. Meanwhile warm the giroles and lentils, heat the sauce and finish with the butter.

To serve, place the lentils onto four warm plates then arrange the giroles around, lay the foie gras on top, spoon the sauce over and around.

BLACK DOOR RESTAURANT

32 Clayton Street West, Newcastle, NE1 5DZ
Tel: 0191 261 6295

BLACK DOOR

Roasted halibut, langoustine lasagne, tomato confit

Serves 4

INGREDIENTS

4 halibut fillets about 170g each, skin on
24 langoustines, shelled
8 baby fennel
2 bags spinach
2kg plum tomatoes

thyme flowers
lasagne sheets
langoustine stock, made from the shells
olive oil

METHOD

For the stock, take 200g seafood shells, 300ml water, sticks each of celery, carrot, fennel, a sprig of basil and a teaspoon of tomato puree. Brown the vegetables and add the shells, water, tomato puree and basil, Simmer for about 20 minutes then put the liquid through a sieve and reduce by half.

For the tomato confit, core and cross each tomato with a knife then plunge them into boiling water for ten seconds, remove and place in iced water. Remove the tomato skins, cut into four and cut away the seeds. Lay the tomato petals onto a lightly oiled tray, sprinkle some thyme flowers and finely sliced garlic onto each one, season, and place in a low oven for three hours to dry out. These oven-dried tomatoes are the confit for the lasagne.

For the fish, in a hot oven, roast the halibut in a little olive oil, flesh side down until golden in colour. Add the langoustines to the pan, cook for one minute and allow to rest. Meanwhile, heat the pasta sheets and cook the spinach and fennel in a little water and butter. Keep warm. Keep two langoustines whole for each plate, the rest can be cut in half lengthways. You can now start to assemble the lasagne.

To serve, layer the pasta sheets with langoustines and tomato. Place the lasagne at the top of the plate with the spinach below. Put the halibut on top and arrange the two whole langoustines and fennel around. Warm the stock sauce and add a knob of butter, then spoon this around the plate.

BLACK DOOR RESTAURANT

32 Clayton Street West, Newcastle, NE1 5DZ
Tel: 0191 261 6295

BLACK DOOR

Chocolate and raspberry mousse with raspberry jelly

INGREDIENTS

CHOCOLATE MOUSSE:

250g milk

250g cream

50g caster sugar

100g egg yolk

200g dark chocolate, 70 cocoa solids

CHOCOLATE SORBET:

400ml milk

100ml water

150g caster sugar

30g cocoa powder

20ml glucose syrup

100g good quality dark chocolate, 70 cocoa solids.

RASPBERRY MOUSSE:

900ml raspberry puree

300ml cream

4 leaves of gelatine

sugar and lemon juice to taste

RASPBERRY JELLY:

100ml raspberry juice

sugar and lemon juice to taste

1^1/$_2$ sheets of leaf gelatine, softened

RASPBERRY SAUCE:

100ml raspberry juice

30g unrefined caster sugar

CHOCOLATE TUILE:

100g egg white

30g cocoa powder

100g flour

50g melted butter

METHOD

For the chocolate mousse, boil milk and cream with sugar, pour onto egg yolks then cool. Strain this onto the chocolate and chill. **For the chocolate sorbet,** boil everything (except the chocolate) for two minutes, pour on to the melted chocolate and chill. Once cool, churn in an ice-cream maker. **For the raspberry jelly,** warm the juice, add the gelatine, sugar and lemon juice and leave to set. **For the raspberry mousse,** warm a little of the puree, add softened gelatine, add this to the rest of the puree. Whip the cream until you have soft peaks then fold it into puree. Add sugar and lemon juice to taste then set aside. **For the raspberry sauce,** reduce juice by half add sugar and boil for one minute; cool. **For the chocolate tuile,** mix all the ingredients together and chill. Spread onto a slightly-oiled baking sheet in rectangular shapes. Bake in a hot oven until bubbles start to appear, take out allow to cool slightly. Remove with a palette knife and mould each tuile around a rolling pin until cool enough to remove. **To serve,** place a small mound of mousse in the centre of the plate then place a scoop of chocolate sorbet on top. Place a tuile on top of this and gently pipe the mousse on top. Cut out the jelly, place a line of sauce across the plate, arrange the jelly and add a few fresh raspberries to finish.

BLACK DOOR RESTAURANT

32 Clayton Street West, Newcastle, NE1 5DZ
Tel: 0191 261 6295

BLACKFRIARS RESTAURANT

BLACKFRIARS
RESTAURANT

With our origins dating back to 1239, Blackfriars Restaurant is the oldest purpose-built restaurant in the UK, with the main restaurant originally built to house the refectory for the 'Black Friars'. The horseshoe of buildings also shelters a medieval courtyard used for *al fresco* dining in the summer.

Blackfriars Restaurant is one of the most recognised restaurants in Newcastle, with its AA rosette, inclusion in the Which? Good Food Guide and Michelin Guide.

Chris Slaughter heads up our kitchen and is a pedigree Northumbrian thoroughbred! He has an enormous passion for seeking out the very best local, organic and seasonal produce – much of it straight from the farm or small artisan producers. His style is firmly rooted in traditional modern British cooking using classic French techniques.

Conversely I didn't enter the hospitality industry until I was in my early thirties, opening Sidney's in 1999. Since then I have nurtured a passion for promoting healthy eating using local, seasonal and organic food, and managing modern British, AA rosette-standard restaurants. I am also a member of Slow Food Newcastle.

Andy Hook, managing director

BLACKFRIARS
RESTAURANT

Seared scallops and foie gras with apple and vanilla chutney, crispy air-dried ham, cider reduction

Serves 4

4 slices of local air-dried ham

APPLE CHUTNEY:

1 vanilla pod, seeded

275ml organic apple juice

1 large Bramley apple, peeled and diced

50g sugar

50g unsalted butter

CIDER REDUCTION:

275ml local organic cider

150g cold unsalted butter

Maldon sea salt and freshly-ground black pepper

SCALLOPS:

olive oil for searing

8 large king scallops cut into 2 discs and seasoned

250g piece of foie gras cut into 4 slices

4 slices of brioche, cut into rounds and toasted

Watercress to garnish

Method, preheat the oven to 160C. Put the air-dried ham onto a baking dish and roast in the oven for around eight minutes until just crisp. **For the apple chutney,** make the apple chutney by adding the vanilla pod (seeds and shell) and sugar to the apple juice. Bring to the boil, allow to infuse for a few minutes before adding the apple. Cook on a low heat until it reaches a chutney consistency. Add the butter at the end, remove the vanilla pod shell, but do not season. **For the cider reduction,** reduce the organic cider by 2/3, whisk in the butter and season. Wipe a tiny amount of oil onto a non-stick frying pan and place on high heat. Place scallops into the pan and fry for one minute on one side until golden. Ensure the pan remains at searing temperature, turn scallops over and add the foie gras to the same pan and cook for a further minute.

To serve, whilst the scallops and foie gras are cooking, drizzle cider reduction onto a warm plate together with a quenelle of chutney. Place on the brioche and scatter pieces of the crispy ham around the plate. Place the foie gras onto the toasted brioche and position four sliced scallops onto the plate. Drizzle a spoon of the foie gras cooking juices on the scallops, garnish with some watercress and serve immediately.

BLACKFRIARS RESTAURANT
Friars Street, Newcastle, NE1 4XN
Tel: 0191 261 5945 www.blackfriarsrestaurant.co.uk

BLACKFRIARS RESTAURANT

Northumbrian organic free-range chicken with horse mushrooms and spinach open lasagne and a roasted garlic sauce

Serves 4

INGREDIENTS

ROAST CHICKEN STOCK:

1 large free-range organic chicken

1 onion, peeled and sliced in half

1 carrot, peeled and cut into quarters

1 leek, washed and trimmed

1 stick celery, washed and trimmed

1 bay leaf

1 sprig of thyme

ROAST GARLIC SAUCE:

Malden sea salt and freshly-ground black pepper

50g unsalted butter

1 small bunch thyme

4 garlic cloves

100ml double cream

oil for browning chicken breasts

LASAGNE:

500g horse mushrooms – cleaned and sliced

knob of butter

250g baby spinach, washed

3 tbsp crème fraiche

12 small fresh lasagne sheets cut into rings and blanched in boiling salted water

Maldon sea salt and freshly-ground black pepper

METHOD

To prepare, set the oven at 140C. Joint the chicken by removing the legs, thighs and breast. **For the roast chicken stock,** roast the carcass in the oven until golden brown and place in a pan with cold water, onion, carrot, bay leaf, sprig of thyme, celery and leek, bring to the boil, skim and simmer for four hours before straining. Season legs and thighs, brown in butter in oven proof pan and then roast in oven for 45 minutes to one hour along with four or so cloves of garlic and thyme. Baste every 10-15 minutes until chicken is sticky, gooey and cooked through. **For the roast garlic sauce,** 'pop' garlic cloves – which should be buttery-soft by now– from their skins to a pan with 200ml of roast chicken stock and reduce by half. Add cream and boil to reduce to a spoon-coating consistency. Whiz up with hand-held mixer. **For the chicken breast,** turn oven up to 180C, season the breasts, brown in a pan and roast for about 10 minutes until cooked through. Rest for 10 minutes before slicing in two at an angle. **For the lasagne,** gently sauté mushrooms in butter, wilt spinach in another pan, drain and mix with mushrooms and crème fraiche. Blanch lasagne discs for a minute in garlic sauce. **To serve,** layer some of the mushroom and spinach mixture onto a warm plate followed by a lasagne disc – repeat with more mixture and second lasagne disc. Place a leg or thigh together with a piece of sliced breast onto the plate and drizzle with remaining roast garlic sauce.

BLACKFRIARS RESTAURANT
Friars Street, Newcastle, NE1 4XN
Tel: 0191 261 5945 www.blackfriarsrestaurant.co.uk

BLACKFRIARS RESTAURANT

Posh fish and chips

Serves 4

INGREDIENTS

sunflower oil for deep-frying

275ml bottle Pilsner lager

2 tbs cornflour

1 tbs white wine vinegar

Maldon sea salt

225g plain flour, plus extra for dusting

TARTARE SAUCE:

small jar of good quality mayonnaise

1 gherkin, finely chopped

1 tbs capers, finely chopped

1 tbs fresh herbs, any combination of chives, chervil and tarragon

CHUNKY CHIPS:

6-8 large floury potatoes, such as Maris Piper, King Edward or Spunter

2 ice cubes

BATTERED FISH:

4 x 175g fillets of very fresh halibut, brill or wild salmon

Maldon sea salt and freshly-ground black pepper

slice of lemon and bunch of watercress

METHOD

Method, preheat oil to 120C. For the beer batter, firstly make the batter by combining the Pilsner, vinegar, corn flour and salt before whisking in the plain flour until the mixture has the consistency of thick double cream, coating the back of a wooden spoon. Chill in fridge for 30 minutes. **For the tartare sauce,** combine all the tartare sauce ingredients together and reserve. **For the chips,** peel the potatoes and cut into large chunky chips. Wash well in cold water, drain and pat dry with a clean tea towel. Blanch gently for about 8-10 minutes, until they are soft but still pale (check they're cooked by piercing with a knife). Lift out of the pan and leave to cool slightly on greaseproof paper. Increase the heat of the fryer to 180C, return the chips to the fryer and cook for 2-3 minutes or until golden and crispy. Drain on kitchen paper and season with salt. **For the battered fish,** remove batter from the fridge and stir in a couple of ice cubes to really chill. Season the fish, dust lightly with flour and thickly coat two of the fillets with the batter. Carefully place in the hot fat and cook for 8-10 minutes until golden and crispy. Remove from the pan and drain on kitchen paper.

To serve, place battered fish and chunky chips on a warmed plate together with a small ramekin of tartare sauce, a wedge of lemon and a small bunch of watercress.

BLACKFRIARS RESTAURANT
Friars Street, Newcastle, NE1 4XN
Tel: 0191 261 5945 www.blackfriarsrestaurant.co.uk

CAFÉ LOWREY

CAFÉ LOWREY

At Café Lowrey our food is deliberately uncomplicated and our aim is to make the best use of the finest fresh, local produce.

I took over the restaurant in April this year, having been head chef there for some years when it was known as Café 21.

It is a labour of love, I know the place well and am continuing the ethos of quality food which I have experienced as a chef working in well-known North East restaurants including Fisherman's Lodge, 21Queen Street, and Bistro 21.

I know and appreciate the importance of creating a warm, relaxed and inviting environment where diners can really enjoy their food and know that it is the best it can be. We strive at Café Lowrey to ensure that this is always the case.

Ian Lowrey, owner, Café Lowrey

CAFÉ LOWREY

Seared scallops with black bean vinaigrette

Serves 4

INGREDIENTS

20 Scottish scallops, cleaned and with roe removed

200g leeks cut into julienne strips and deep fried

VINAIGRETTE:

100g salted black beans

100g shallots, very finely chopped

50g ginger, very finely chopped

1 garlic clove, very finely chopped

300ml extra virgin olive oil

150ml light soy sauce

METHOD

To prepare, pour two tablespoons of olive oil into a frying pan. Season the scallops with salt and pepper and make sure the frying pan is very hot. Add the scallops and cook for a minute either side, making sure they are golden brown. Add a knob of butter and a squeeze of lemon juice. Remove immediately to prevent overcooking. Place the scallops on a plate, warm the vinaigrette, pour over the scallops and place deep fried leeks on top.

CAFÉ LOWREY

33-35 The Broadway, Darras Hall, Ponteland, NE20 9PW
Tel: 01661 820357, www.cafelowrey.co.uk

CAFÉ LOWREY

Confit of duck with Lyonnaise potatoes and fine French beans, thyme and rosemary butter

Serves 4

INGREDIENTS

4 large confit duck legs (confit is duck preserved in fat, available in delis and some supermarkets)

duck fat from the above

8 large potatoes, preferably Charlotte, sliced into rounds

6 small onions, finely diced

50g thyme, finely chopped

30ml olive oil

400g extra fine French beans

* ½ pint veal jus

250g butter

50g thyme

50g rosemary

METHOD

To prepare, place the duck legs in a hot oven until crispy and brown. Sauté potatoes in duck fat until coloured either side. Cook unions in duck fat until soft and golden. Add thyme to the onions then mix potatoes and onions together and place on a warmed plate. Cook the French beans for two minutes in boiling water. Place the beans at the side of the Lyonnaise potatoes and place the duck confit on top. Heat the veal jus to reduce, add thyme and rosemary butter. Pour around the duck.

* To make the jus, make a stock with two carrots, an onion, a leek, two sticks of celery and half a garlic bulb, 200g tomato puree, 2kg veal bones, 500ml white wine and 3-4 litres of water. Simmer for about three hours then strain the liquid and retain. Reduce it to a gravy-like consistency to serve.

CAFÉ LOWREY

Lemon tart

Serves 12

INGREDIENTS

SWEET SHORTCRUST PASTRY:

200g plain flour

100g butter, diced

75g caster sugar

1 egg

25ml milk

TART FILLING:

4 eggs

1 egg yolk

250g caster sugar

200ml lemon puree

250ml double cream

icing sugar to decorate

METHOD

For the pastry, sift flour and rub the butter into the flour until it resembles breadcrumbs; add the sugar. Beat the egg and milk and work gently into the crumbs to form a smooth dough. Wrap in clingfilm and place in the fridge for 20-30 minutes before using. Line a baking case with pastry then bake blind for about 15 minutes at 160C.

For the tart filling, whisk eggs and sugar until pale. Slowly add the lemon puree then the cream. Pass through a fine sieve then add to the blind baked pastry case. Cook in the oven set to 180C for about 30 minutes or until set in the middle. Leave to cool then place in the fridge to set.

To serve, sprinkle the top with icing sugar and serve with fresh raspberries.

CAFÉ LOWREY

33-35 The Broadway, Darras Hall, Ponteland, NE20 9PW
Tel: 01661 820357, www.cafelowrey.co.uk

CLOSE HOUSE
COUNTRY CLUB

CLOSE HOUSE
COUNTRY CLUB

Close House Country Club is fast becoming one of the most up-and-coming places to eat in the North East. Set in 300 acres of wooded grounds just 15 miles from the city centre, the luxurious Close House has established an exceptional reputation for its restaurant since opening earlier this year. My team offers guests traditional seasonal cuisine with a French influence in the intimately decorated restaurant, as well as a selection of snacks, fine wines and cocktails in the cocktail lounge and bar.

My aim is to use my wide experience in cooking to provide customers with the best ingredients possible and we are committed to using the freshest produce available whether that is locally sourced or from across Western Europe. The extensive menu includes imaginative dishes with a generous wine list to complement the high quality food and service that makes up the exquisite experience that is Close House dining.

Tony Binks, head chef

Corn-fed chicken, duck liver and wild mushroom terrine

Serves 4

INGREDIENTS

6 corn-fed chicken legs	sliced Bayonne or Parma ham to line
sea salt	terrine mould
500g duck fat	10g chopped shallots
500g duck livers and 200g unsalted	10g chopped fresh tarragon or parsley
butter *or* 500g fresh duck foie gras	10g crushed garlic
200gm cleaned mixed wild	nutmeg
or domestic mushrooms	salt and pepper to season

METHOD

To prepare, marinate chicken legs in sea salt for 24 hours in refrigerator. Remove excess salt with damp cloth. Melt the duck fat and cook chicken legs immersed in the duck fat for 2^1/$_2$-3 hours, 110-120C, until chicken can be removed from the bone easily. Remove legs from fat and allow to cool until it can be handled. Remove all skin and bone, flake all meat and keep warm.

If using foie gras, cut the liver into equal portions, about 2cm nuggets. Allow liver to warm to room temperature and sauté in frying pan on all sides until brown, season with salt and pepper, this will take two or three minutes. The liver should be soft in the centre – large amounts of duck fat will melt into the pan, but this is normal. Remove the liver and add to the warm chicken meat. Retain the duck foie gras fat to sauté the wild mushrooms, shallots, herbs and garlic, and add the contents of the pan to the chicken and liver mix. If using duck livers sauté in all the butter, keeping the livers pink using the butter as a replacement for the foie gras fat.

Line your terrine mould with cling film and then the parma ham, mix all ingredients well and press into terrine mould. Line the top of terrine with ham then wrap the whole terrine in cling film, place suitable weights on top and press terrine for 24 hours in refrigerator. This terrine can then be sliced, served at room temperature with home made chutney and toasted country bread.

Baked chicken supreme with wild mushrooms and tarragon in red wine jus

Serves 4

INGREDIENTS

CHICKEN MOUSSE:

250g chicken fillet (fully trimmed, diced and chilled)

1 egg white

250ml double cream

50g mixed wild mushrooms (washed and diced)

25g chopped shallots

15g chopped fresh tarragon

10g butter

salt, pepper and nutmeg to season

CHICKEN SUPREME:

4 chicken supremes (skin remaining, clean the wing bone or remove and trim excess fat)

250ml fresh brown chicken stock

250ml red wine

25g unsalted butter

25g chopped shallots

2 sprigs fresh thyme

METHOD

For the mousse, sauté chopped shallots in butter until cooked, but without colour, add chopped mushrooms and cook until tender. Stir in chopped tarragon, season with salt and pepper and chill. Place the chilled chicken fillet and egg whites into a food processor and process until very smooth. This can then be left to chill for ten minutes to relax the protein in the chicken. When chilled add the cream in three stages – it is best to do this using the pulse switch on your food processor. Ensure the cream is blended evenly - the mousse should resemble slightly melted ice-cream. Season with salt, pepper and nutmeg and fold in the cooked mushrooms and chill once again. The chilling and the salt will firm the mousse ready for the next process. **For the chicken,** place the supremes skin down and insert a small sharp knife into the knuckle end of the chicken, pushing the blade as deep as possible without splitting the sides, keeping the opening as small as possible. This creates a pocket which can be filled with the cold chicken mousse, best achieved by using a piping bag to push the mousse into the supreme. Place the stuffed chicken onto a buttered ovenproof dish and season. Brush the chicken skin with melted butter and bake for 12-15 mins, at 180C. Remove from the oven and keep chicken warm, retaining the pan juices. **For the sauce,** sauté shallots in half the butter, add the pan juices and red wine. Bring to simmer and reduce the liquid by half. Add thyme and chicken stock, simmer and reduce by two-thirds. Remove from heat and add the remaining butter using a whisk until smooth, pass sauce through a fine sieve and serve hot over the stuffed chicken.

CLOSE HOUSE COUNTRY CLUB
Close House, Heddon-on-the-Wall, Newcastle, NE15 0HT
Tel: 01661 852255 www.closehouse.co.uk

75

CLOSE HOUSE
COUNTRY CLUB

Baked lemon tart with praline cream and fresh raspberries

Serves 4

INGREDIENTS

25g butter for greasing

600g sweet pastry

4 large lemons

8 eggs

375g caster sugar

300ml double cream

100g icing sugar

1 punnet fresh raspberries

250ml double cream (whipped)

100g praline or hazelnut brittle (broken in a food processor)

sprigs of mint

METHOD

To prepare, butter a 22cm flan ring. Roll out the sweet pastry to approx 4mm and line ring, ensuring you trim excess pastry and crimp edges. Line flan with silicon paper and fill with baking beans. Blind bake the case in a pre-heated oven, 160C, for 12-15 minutes. Remove baking beans and silicon paper from the tart but leave it in the flan ring. Sprinkle the base of the tart with half of the icing sugar and using a blow torch caramelise the base of the tart, which helps keep it crisp.

Zest the lemons, squeeze and sieve the juice. Break the eggs into a bowl, add the sugar, whisk until smooth and add lemon juice and lemon zest. Boil the double cream and slowly pour over the eggs and lemons, whisking throughout. Return the liquid to a clean thick-bottomed sauce pan and return to the heat. Cook gently, stirring with a spatula until thick and creamy; this should not boil or it may curdle and split. Pour the warm custard into the flan case and cook in the oven for 12 minutes at 150C to finish cooking the custard. Remove from the oven and allow to cool, but do not refrigerate. Allow to stand for 2-3 hours. Sprinkle remaining icing sugar over the tart and again caramelise using a blow torch – this gives great texture.

Serve with fresh raspberries, praline cream and fresh mint.

CLOSE HOUSE COUNTRY CLUB

Close House, Heddon-on-the-Wall, Newcastle, NE15 0HT
Tel: 01661 852255 www.closehouse.co.uk

CRAB & LOBSTER

CRAB & LOBSTER

Here at the Crab & Lobster we believe in good, honest food served in comfortable, relaxed surroundings. I suppose you might describe our dishes as modern European with a twist – nothing intricate, just simple food cooked in a creative way and using the best produce of the day.

I've been here for 14 years now, and with the support of a strong, dedicated team I am proud to have built a reputation for excellent food. We specialise in fish, which is delivered twice a day, six days a week, much of it from the North East coast. Among the fish lovers' favourites is our medallions of monkfish, braised leeks, brown shrimps and Beaujolais sauce.

We also look after carnivores, with dishes such as our slowly-braised Moroccan spiced lamb shank, and vegetarians with dishes such as thin tart of goat's cheese with tomato and red onion. I've been a chef for 33 years and believe that the food we're producing is among the best in the region, so I hope you'll enjoy trying it for yourself!

Stephen Dean, head chef

CRAB & LOBSTER

Twice-baked Ribblesdale goats cheese soufflé with orange, carrot and chervil salad

Serves 4

INGREDIENTS

150g Ribblesdale goats cheese, diced small

4 large eggs, separated

40g butter

40g plain flour

1 tsp English mustard

200ml milk

1 small onion, finely chopped

1 pinch ground nutmeg seasoning

SALAD:

selection of salad leaves

pinch of fresh chopped chervil

preferred vinaigrette dressing

2 medium carrots

juice of 2 oranges

METHOD

For the soufflés, pre heat oven to 180C and lightly grease four tea cups. Heat milk in a pan with the finely chopped onion and bring to just below boiling. Strain into a jug and discard the onion. Heat butter in pan and add flour and mustard. Mix well then cook on a low heat for 30 seconds, add the warm milk gradually and mix vigorously until thick and glossy. Fold in diced goats cheese and allow to cool for five minutes. Whisk egg whites until stiff and carefully fold into the base mix. Fill tea cups approx $^2/_3$ full, place in a suitably sized roasting tray that has been $^1/_2$ filled with hot water, and place in the oven for 15-20 minutes until soufflés have risen, goldened and set. Allow the soufflés to cool and sink slightly, then turn out onto a tray-cooling rack. They will be fine in the fridge for a couple of days before use. Preheat the oven to 200C. Place soufflés upside down on a buttered tray and cook for five minutes to puff up. Serve on the salad.

For the salad, arrange a selection of salad leaves then add a pinch of fresh chopped chervil, your preferred vinaigrette dressing, carrots which have been peeled, grated then lightly braised in the juice of two oranges for 2-3 minutes and allowed to cool. Whisk any remaining orange juice from the carrots into the vinaigrette and serve.

Roast local cod chunk with Thai crab risotto and a lime and ginger relish

Serves 4

INGREDIENTS

4 200g cod chunks	If you can't get bones, use fish stock
150g risotto rice	cubes,1 per pint)
100g butter	1 large onion, peeled and quartered
1 red onion, peeled and chopped	2 carrots, peeled and chopped
1 bunch spring onions, finely chopped	4 celery sticks
1 red chilli	6 whole white peppercorns
zest and juice of 2 limes	2 bay leaves
1 garlic clove, finely chopped	1 fennel bulb, halved
1 tsp fine chopped, blanched fresh ginger	1 glass dry white wine (optional)
3 tbs groundnut or corn oil	
50g fresh dressed crab meat	**LIME AND GINGER RELISH:**
50g creamed coconut block	4 limes, zest and segments
pinch fresh chopped coriander	1 shallot, finely chopped
seasoning	1 garlic clove, finely chopped
	1 tsp green ginger wine
FISH STOCK:	1 dsp lime marmalade
450g fish bones (ideally white flat fish.	½ tsp fine chopped, blanched ginger

METHOD

For best results, make the relish and stock a day before. **For the fish stock,** put all ingredients in a large pan, cover with two litres of cold water, bring to boil, simmer and skim off scum as it comes to surface. Lower heat and gently simmer for 15 minutes. Strain and refrigerate. **For the relish,** gently sweat onions and garlic for 2-3 minutes, add all other ingredients and bring to the boil. Gently simmer for five minutes and place in fridge to cool and set. **For the risotto,** heat the remaining butter and oil in a good size heavy-bottomed pan. Gently fry the onions, garlic and lime for 3-4 minutes until soft. Add the rice, take off the heat and stir everything together well. Return to heat and add fish stock gradually – just enough to cover the mixture – and simmer, stirring all the time until liquid has been absorbed. Continue to add more stock as previously until all stock is used. The rice should have a creamy coating but be slightly *al denté*. To finish, break in creamy coconut block and fold in chopped coriander and crab meat. Heat a frying pan with 1 tbs of oil and colour cod pieces on sides and bottom. Transfer to lightly buttered roasting dish and season well. Leave for 3-4 minutes before placing in a pre heated oven at 200C. Cook for 10-12 minutes depending on the thickness of fish – it will be firm to the touch when cooked. Place the risotto on warm plates with the cod and a dessert spoonful of lime relish then serve.

CRAB & LOBSTER

Warm chocolate tart with vanilla mascarpone

Serves 4

INGREDIENTS

150g unsalted butter for pastry
75g caster sugar
100g cocoa powder
150g plain flour
2 egg yolks
1/2 egg white

MASCARPONE CREAM:
125g mascarpone

30g icing sugar
1 vanilla pod

FILLING:
100g good quality dark chocolate
100g salted butter
3 eggs
100g caster sugar
45g plain flour

METHOD

For the pastry, cream butter and sugar together then sift cocoa powder and flour and add to the butter and sugar mixture. Mix well. Add egg, mix and blend. Roll out pastry, line 16 x 8cm cases, bake blind in a preheated oven at 180C for 8mins, remove and cool.

For the filling, gently melt chocolate and butter, whisk eggs and sugar till pale in colour, mix the egg and chocolate mixture together and carefully incorporate the flour with a spatula. Fill pastry cases, place in oven for 10-12 minutes at 180C. Serve straight away – the centre should be slightly runny, similar to a fondant.

For mascarpone cream, beat together the mascarpone, icing sugar and vanilla seeds from pod, then scoop onto the chocolate tarts using a spoon which has been immersed in hot water.

CRAB & LOBSTER

Dishforth Road, Asenby, near Thirsk, YO7 3QL
Tel: 01845 577286 www.crabandlobster.co.uk

CRATHORNE HALL

CRATHORNE HALL

Crathorne Hall Hotel is an example of fine Edwardian architecture and is the former home to the Dugdale family. As part of the Handpicked Collection of Hotels (AA Hotel Group of the year 2004/2005), good food and wine is the core value of the group, no where more so than at Crathorne, where the tradition of entertaining can still be enjoyed in our Leven Restaurant, in a somewhat more relaxed style than in years gone by.

After a successful stint L'Horizon in Jersey, another of the Handpicked Collection, Peter Fleming our award winning Executive Head Chef has now returned to the mainland and has settled down in North Yorkshire. Using some of the finest local ingredience and produce, Peter is creating a fine traditional cuisine with a well-balanced and enjoyable dining experience.

With his already formidable reputation, Peter has introduced a successful gourmet club and in 2006 he will host a series of cookery demonstrations at the hotel. This will re-establish the traditions of fine dining to the Leven Restaurant, as it is Peter's aim to ensure that Crathorne Hall has a reputation as one of the most successful North East restaurants.

Peter Fleming, head chef

CRATHORNE HALL

Pan fried fillet of wild sea bass with basil mash and fine ratatouille set on shell fish froth

Serves 4

INGREDIENTS

1 whole 600g wild sea bass (ask your fishmonger to clean and fillet it) cut into four portions

2 large maris piper potatoes

30g fresh basil

olive oil

shellfish bones (lobster or crab)

1/2 pt double cream

seasoning

1 small glass brandy

RATATOUILLE:

1 courgette

1 aubergine

2 plum tomatoes

1 red onion

1 garlic clove

1 red pepper

METHOD

To prepare, finely dice all the ingredients for the ratatouille and cook in a small amount of olive oil until tender. Keep warm. Roast the shellfish bones off in a hot oven until brittle. Add brandy and cream and trimmings from the ratatouille vegetables to the fishbones for flavour. Reduce then pass through a sieve to leave a light, creamy fish sauce. Boil potatoes, mash, and blend with olive oil, basil and puree in a food processor. Keep warm. Cook the fish for two minutes each side in a very hot pan with oil. Season and serve.

CRATHORNE HALL

Crathorne, Yarm, North Yorkshire, TS15 OAR
Tel: 01642 700398 www.handpicked.co.uk

Grilled fillet of Scotch beef with forestierre sauce

Serves 4

INGREDIENTS

4 x 220g Scotch beef fillets

12 small shallots

125g wild mushrooms

50g pancetta cut into matchstick size strips

1/4 of a celeriac

12 small potatoes (cubed or turned)

1/4 pt beef or veal jus (ready bought)

1 glass red wine

oil

25g butter

5g sugar

1 garlic clove

flat parsley sprig, chopped

seasoning

1/4 pint milk

METHOD

To prepare, cook shallots in red wine, butter, and sugar until tender (cover pan with foil). Cook celeriac in milk and puree. Cover and keep warm. Fry potatoes in oil till golden brown and tender. Griddle fillet steaks, or pan fry until cooked to your liking, then let them rest for five to eight minutes. Pan fry mushrooms, pancetta and garlic, season to taste and add parsley when cooked. Serve with jus.

CRATHORNE HALL

Crathorne, Yarm, North Yorkshire, TS15 OAR
Tel: 01642 700398 www.handpicked.co.uk

Chocolate fondant

Serves 4

INGREDIENTS

200g bitter chocolate
200g butter
4 whole eggs
4 egg yolks
100g sugar
57g soft flour
Pinch salt

MILK ICE CREAM:

300g wholemilk, reduced to 280g
130g condensed milk
10g glucose

METHOD

For the chocolate fondant, melt butter and chocolate over a bain marie, not exceeding 40C. Whisk eggs and sugar to ribbon stage. Fold the chocolate and egg mix together. Fold this in flour. Place into a well-buttered mould. Bake at 180C for eight minutes and leave to rest for two minutes.

For the milk ice cream, heat and reduce milk to 280g and add condensed milk and glucose. Churn two or three times and freeze. Alternatively use an ice cream maker.

THE FEVERSHAM
ARMS HOTEL

THE FEVERSHAM
ARMS HOTEL

At the Feversham Arms, we cook what we sometimes refer to as real food. Dishes that belong here in the North Yorkshire Moors, imbued with the quality of ingredients we enjoy in this region, in a style that most of us recognise. We don't think that quality has to be complicated - but we can do that too when it's right for the dish. Game, lamb and seafood from nearby Whitby are perennial favourites, complemented by a wine list of over two hundred bins.

Our conservatory restaurant is the heart of the hotel. It's a place where you won't have to whisper and buzzes with life on busy evenings. Here, you'll find that eclectic, personal, mix of modern and old mix that has become our trademark, where Julia Burns' contemporary paintings sit comfortable above Mouseman furniture.

On Summer days, enjoy drinks in our poolside garden before or after lunch.

We also serve afternoon tea throughout the year - in the Summer by the pool - or in Winter by the fire.

Charlie Lakin, head chef

Asparagus Salad

Serves 4

INGREDIENTS

16 spears of asparagus
8 baby carrots
50g garden peas
50g broad beans
150g Jersey Royal potatoes
4 quail eggs
1 cup of fine bread crumbs
Fine salad leaves

CREAMED TRUFFLE DRESSING:

100ml ground nut oil
50 ml white truffle oil
25ml white wine vinegar
26ml sherry vinegar
40ml double cream
10g fine chopped fresh truffle
1 teaspoon chopped thyme

METHOD

To prepare, first peel and trim asparagus and baby carrots, set to a side. Clean Jersey Royals and cook in boiling water with a quarter of a lemon and a clove of garlic. Blanche asparagus and baby carrots in heavily salted water. Drain any excess water and set aside with other vegetables. Boil the quail eggs for 1 minute, 40 seconds and cool in iced water. Gently peel the quail eggs, which is tricky, so you may need to use two per person, in case of breakages. Then cover the eggs in flour, egg and then the fine breadcrumbs, set aside.

For the dressing, whisk the oils and vinegar together, add the chopped truffle and thyme, lastly add the cream and liquidise with a stick blender to emulsify the dressing, (any excess can be kept in the fridge for up to 4 days).

To arrange the salad, first, finely slice the potatoes and lightly dress, arrange in an overlapped circle in the middle of your plates, about 5 – 6 slices per person. Place 3 spears of asparagus in a triangle on top of the potatoes, slice the remaining asparagus and baby carrots, mix with the peas beans and leaves, season and lightly dressing arrange on top of the asparagus, lastly deep fry the quail egg till golden brown and place on top, lightly drizzle some dressing on the plate.

THE FEVERSHAM ARMS HOTEL

Loin of Rabbit

Serves 4

INGREDIENTS

2 whole Rabbits	2 Potatoes (preferably Desiree or Marfona)
75g Black Pudding	
1 Shallot – finely diced	1 pt Veal stock
1 tsp chopped thyme	1/4 pt of apple juice
1 small celeriac	1 good sprig of lovage
2 Granny Smiths apples	12 baby carrots (cooked)
75g melted butter	12 baby leeks (cooked)

Method, firstly remove the loins, with the belly still attached (as this will be required to wrap the loins later), legs and kidneys. Roast the remaining bones to make a stock, to make the sauce. Cover the rabbit bones with water, with 1/2 an onion, 1 carrot, a stick of celery and a bay leaf, bring to the boil and then simmer for 4 hours. Strain and add the veal stock, apple juice and lovage, reduce by 2/3 until the sauce lightly covers the back of the spoon, pass through a fine sieve and set to one side. Remove the meat from the legs, trimming any excess fat and sinews from it and dice into small chunks. Also dice the black pudding, add to the rabbit, along with the shallots and thyme, process to make a course stuffing and season. Lay the loins with the belly still attached, flat onto cling-film and divide the stuffing between the 4 loins, place on the inside next to the loin, then roll inside the belly flap forming a sausage shape. Tightly roll each loin in cling and tie the ends to set the shape and make it easier to cook.

For the galettes, finely slice the potatoes, apples and celeriac using individual tart cases, line each one with a circle of silicone paper and a spoon of melted butter. Fan the finely sliced potato around the base, just one layer, then celeriac, then apple, gently season. Keep doing this until you have 4 layers of apple and then top with a layer of potato in a pinwheel pattern. Cover in butter and cook in the oven at 170c for 20 mins or until they can be gently pierced with a knife.

Unwrap, the rabbit loins out of cling film and tie with string to stop them popping open during cooking. Gently seal off in a heavy based pan until golden all over and place in the oven for 5-6 mins, remove and leave to rest.

To serve, arrange the galettes in the middle of four plates, reheat the baby vegetables in butter and water, arrange around the galette. Slice the rabbit into 6 and fan on top of the galette, lightly sauté off the kidneys for 45 seconds each side, slice and place on the top then spoon the warm finished sauce around the outside.

THE FEVERSHAM ARMS HOTEL

Helmsley, North Yorkshire, YO62 5AG
Tel : 01439 770766   www.fevershamarmshotel.com

THE FEVERSHAM ARMS HOTEL

Chocolate & Horlicks Parfait

Makes 10

BITTER CHOCOLATE PARFAIT:

275g Dark Chocolate

4 Egg Whites

50g Castor Sugar

50g Icing Sugar

Pinch of Cream of Tartar

200ml Whipped Cream

HORLICKS PARFAIT:

1 pint of Cream

1 pint of Milk

1 dessert spoon of Glucose Syrup

225g Chocolate Horlicks

10 egg yolks

50g Sugar

BANANA COMPOTE:

1 Banana

35g crushed hazelnuts

1 dessert spoon of melted chocolate

1/2 measure of Baileys

1 dessert spoon Toffee Sauce

Firstly, melt the chocolate. Whisk the egg whites, sugars and cream of tartar to form a meringue. Fold the meringue into the melted chocolate, then gently fold in the whipped cream. Fill your moulds 1/2 full and freeze

Next the Horlicks Parfait, first boil the cream, milk, glucose and Horlicks. Beat egg yolks and sugar until smooth and then gradually add to the cream, constantly stirring to avoid the eggs curdling. Leave to cool, then churn through the ice-cream machine. When set, top the moulds off and place back in the freezer to set.

For the compote, dice the banana fine, then bind together all the ingredients and place in the fridge to set.

To plate, dip the moulds into hot water and turn out onto crushed nuts, then turn over onto the centre of the plate, then place three quenelles of the banana round the parfait, serve instantly to avoid the parfait melting.

THE FEVERSHAM ARMS HOTEL

Helmsley, North Yorkshire, YO62 5AG
Tel : 01439 770766 www.fevershamarmshotel.com

FISHERMAN'S LODGE

FISHERMAN'S LODGE

Hidden in Jesmond Dene, a small woodland valley five minutes from the centre of Newcastle, Fisherman's Lodge is a haven of calm and one of the city's finest restaurants. Stylish, elegant and spacious, it's the home of exquisitely prepared traditional and modern dishes.

Serving the freshest fish, delivered daily from the quay at North Shields. More exotic dishes such as hand-dived scallops are brought in from the Isle of Skye, while lobster, red snapper and monkfish are now also sourced locally.

But it's not all fish. Northumbrian lamb, beef and venison are sourced from the best growers in the area.

As for our sweets, well who could resist such treats as blueberry souffle with vanilla and blueberry ripple parfait or mille-feuille of Bramley apple compote with mascarpone cheese sorbet?

As for the cheese, each one is selected with care. Try tartufo, a pecorino-style cheese studded with truffles, or epoisses, the most pungent cheese in the world.

Great food in great style.

Jamie Walsh, head chef

FISHERMAN'S LODGE

Seared king scallops with crushed peas, pancetta and shallot puree

Serves 4

INGREDIENTS

6 king scallops, prepared by your fishmonger

9 rashers pancetta

200g fresh peas

1 tbs chicken stock

2 tbs olive oil

small knob butter

400g shallots, finely chopped

4 tbs double cream

salt and pepper

250ml Barolo red wine

125ml port

METHOD

To prepare, pre-heat the oven to 200C. Slice the scallops into medallions and sear on both sides in a hot frying pan for 45 seconds until golden brown. Place the pancetta on two non-stick trays and cook in the oven for four minutes or until crispy then cut into 1cm by 5cm strips. For the pea puree, blanch peas in boiling water for 20-30 seconds, drain and add chicken stock then blitz in a food processor to leave a rustic rather than smooth texture. Season with salt and pepper.

For the shallot puree, warm the olive oil and butter in a saucepan and add 325g of shallots. Cover and cook over a gentle heat for 15 minutes without allowing it to colour. Add three or four tablespoons of water to the shallots once they begin to soften. Add the cream and continue to cook for a further five minutes. Remove from heat and season well. Liquidise to a smooth puree.

For Barolo sauce, mix the Barolo wine and port in a saucepan and reduce by half until a thick syrup. For shallot confit, sweat the remaining shallots in a saucepan with butter until golden brown and soft.

To serve, place three teaspoons of pea puree parallel to the edge of the plate, just off centre. Pipe one line of shallot puree and one line of Barolo sauce beneath the pea puree. At one end of the plate, arrange three small heaps of the shallot confit. At the last minute, place the scallops on top of the pea puree and garnish with pancetta.

FISHERMAN'S LODGE

Deep Dene House, Jesmond Dene, Newcastle, NE7 7BQ
Tel: 0191 281 3281   www.tomscompanies.com

FISHERMAN'S LODGE

Roast loin of venison, braised savoy cabbage, squash, chestnuts, Sarladaise potatoes and red wine jus

Serves 4

INGREDIENTS

4 120g venison loins

MARINADE:
olive oil
2 cloves garlic
2 sprigs thyme
2 bay leaves
mix ingredients together

SARLADAISE POTATOES:
4 half-cooked jacket potatoes, skins remove and flesh grated
20g diced pancetta
10g chopped thyme
10ml duck fat

BRAISED SAVOY CABBAGE:
1 butternut squash, diced
1 packet pre-cooked chestnuts
1 Savoy cabbage
200ml red wine jus

METHOD

To prepare, place venison in the marinade and leave for 24 hours. To make the sarladaise potatoes, put the ingredients in a bowl and mix together. Place approx 200g of the potato mix into a cake shape and bake in the oven for 10 minutes until golden, brown in duck fat. Then bake in oven for 10 minutes. Seal off the meat in a hot pan then place in the oven for six-eight minutes. Finely shred the cabbage and braise in stock until tender. Fry the pumpkin and chestnuts in butter.

To serve, place the potato and cabbage at opposite ends of the plate with venison slice on top of the cabbage. Garnish with chestnuts and pumpkin, heat the sauce and serve.

FISHERMAN'S LODGE

Deep Dene House, Jesmond Dene, Newcastle, NE7 7BQ
Tel: 0191 281 3281   www.tomscompanies.com

FISHERMAN'S LODGE

Iced Valhrona milk chocolate parfait

Serves 4

INGREDIENTS

5 egg yolks

125g caster sugar

50ml Baileys Irish Cream liqueur

200g Valhrona milk chocolate
(42% solids)

350ml double cream, whipped

METHOD

Method, whisk yolks and sugar over a bain-marie until thick and a ribbon-like consistency. Add Baileys then chocolate. Gently fold in the whipped cream. Pour into moulds and freeze for at least three hours.

* At the restaurant we serve it with white chocolate mousse, caramel strands, choux pastry lattice and a dentelle wafer.

FISHERMAN'S LODGE

Deep Dene House, Jesmond Dene, Newcastle, NE7 7BQ
Tel: 0191 281 3281 www.tomscompanies.com

GISBOROUGH HALL

GISBOROUGH HALL

Here in the kitchens at Gisborough Hall we are very fortunate to have access to Lord Gisborough's marvellous kitchen garden.

It is an enviable resource and one which inspires all the chefs on my team, because it means we are able to source the freshest herbs and in-season vegetables at all times. This freshness and attention to detail is the starting point for every dish served in the hotel's restaurant.

Fine local produce such as Richmond beef, North Yorkshire Moors game or Whitby crab is the best tool a chef can have, and such quality ingredients are the cornerstone of our cooking.

More than ever before people are asking about the source of their food and its seasonality. They are demanding the best. We are lucky that such fine produce is on our doorstep and the challenge of creating the best dishes is one which always excites a chef and his team.

Jason Moore, head chef

GISBOROUGH HALL

Crispy belly pork with Asian salad

Serves 4

INGREDIENTS

500g sliced belly pork

2 red chillies

3 garlic cloves, crushed

25g fresh ginger, peeled

1 lemon, halved

1 lime, halved

2 tsp ground cumin

2 tsp coriander seeds

DRESSING:

sweet chilli sauce

toasted sesame seeds

fresh chopped coriander

ASIAN SALAD:

julienne (thin strips) of:

carrot

courgette

leek

red and yellow peppers

mooli (japanese radish available from

supermarkets and greengrocers)

METHOD

To prepare, place the meat ingredients into a pan, cover with water and bring to the boil. Simmer until tender. Once tender, drain and cool. When cooled, remove the belly pork meat.

For the salad, Place the ingredients in ice-cold water for at least 30 minutes. This will make the salad very crisp.

To serve, place the belly pork into a deep fat fryer at 180C until crispy then remove and drain on a paper towel. Roll the crispy belly pork in dressing and serve in a bowl, topped with Asian salad.

GISBOROUGH HALL

Roast venison with fondant potato, turned vegetables, spinach and a girole mushroom sauce

Serves 4

INGREDIENTS

4 x 200g venison rack

4 large potatoes

2 large carrots

2 large courgettes

1 celeriac

spinach

300g girole mushrooms or wild mix mushrooms

200ml red wine sauce

METHOD

To prepare, take potatoes and cut into cylinder shapes. Place in a roasting tray, half cover with vegetable stock and place a knob of butter on each one and place in a pre-eated oven at 180C for about 20 minutes, or until tender. Remove from the oven and allow to cool. Peel and cut the carrots into two and shape into barrels. Cut courgettes into two and shape into barrels. Peel and cut the celeriac into four and shape into barrels. Cook each of the vegetables in boiling salted water until tender then remove and place into ice cold water to refresh the vegetables. These vegetables can be prepared the day before.

Take the venison and season well with salt and pepper. Take af frying pan and heat until very hot,adding some vegetable oil. Seal the venison on all cides until nicely browned, remove from the pan, place on a baking tray and put in a pre-heated oven at 200C with the cold fondant potatoes for 12 minutes. Return the venison pan to the heat and sauté the mushrooms in the meat juices. When cooked, place them on a paper towel. Place spinach in a pan of boiling salted water for 30 seconds, remove from the water and drain in a sieve, then set aside and keep warm. Place the carrots, courgettes and celeriac into boiling salted water for two minutes, remove, then mix with the spinch and keep warm. Bring red wine sauce to the boil and add mushrooms and seasoning.

To serve, remove the venison and potatoes from the oven and allow to stand for a minute or two as you put the vegetables and potatoes on a plate, then slice the meat into three for each plate, and finish with mushroom sauce.

GISBOROUGH HALL

Whitby Lane, Guisborough, North Yorkshire, TS14 6PT
Tel: 0870 400 8191 www.gisborough-hall.co.uk

GISBOROUGH HALL

Mango and passionfruit cheesecake with kumquat and lychee syrup

Serves 4

INGREDIENTS

10-inch springform pan lined with parchment paper

250g digestive biscuits

100g demerera sugar

125g melted butter

FILLING:

2 ripe mangoes

200g caster sugar

200ml water

4 leaves of gelatine soaked in cold water

12 passionfruit, flesh and seeds scooped out

$^1/_2$ lt double cream, three-quarters whipped.

500g cream cheese

SYRUP:

12 lychees

12 kumquats

3 x 200ml water

3 x 200g caster sugar

METHOD

For the base, in a food processor, mix biscuits and sugar to a fine crumb. Mix in melted butter until well incorporated. Press into the bottom of the pan to form a smooth base, then refrigerate.

For the filling, cook mangoes, caster sugar and water in a pan until the mangoes are soft. Puree in a blender until smooth. Add passionfruit pulp then drained, squeezed gelatine leaves. Mix well with a wooden spoon. Cool the mixture, but do not refrigerate. Fold together the cream cheese and whipped cream and then fold in the cooled fruit mixture. Pour onto the biscuit base and chill.

For the syrup, the kumquats need softening by poaching at least three times. To do this, place the water, sugar and fruit in a pan and bring to a simmer. As they reach simmer, toss the fruit into iced water then throw away the syrup. Repeat this three times, retaining the final batch of syrup. The lychees need peeling and pitting to remove stones. Then they too are added to the syrup.

To serve, when the cheesecake is cold you can top it with a little fruit puree mixed with a couple of leaves of gelatine, soaked in water then rinsed and squeezed, to give a glossy finish.

GISBOROUGH HALL

Whitby Lane, Guisborough, North Yorkshire, TS14 6PT
Tel: 0870 400 8191 www.gisborough-hall.co.uk

GREENS

Greens

· Licensed Restaurant ·

Tel:
(01947) 600284

Greens

·Licensed R

GREENS

I can't think of a better place to live and work than Whitby, that can provide all that we need to offer visitors to our restaurant – the best of everything local. Our menu reflects this in every way. Our fish is sourced right down to the names of the trawlers coming into Whitby Harbour, a few steps away from our restaurant. We visit the farms that supply our butcher to choose the best of their livestock. Vegetables and herbs are from local suppliers and are delivered directly to us, so they don't have that travel-weary look about them! And our cheese menu includes many local options. This gives us a great deal of satisfaction – we know that when you visit Greens your food will be cooked in a style that lets the freshest of ingredients speak for themselves, without too many embellishments, so that you can taste the heart of the dish. The atmosphere is warm and welcoming.

Deep red walls, soft lighting, wood panelling. An altogether relaxing experience. We are extremely proud to be in the new Egon Ronay Top 200 restaurants in the UK guide, plus being winners of the 'Discover Yorkshire Coast Tourism Awards 2005' as Best Restaurant/Café Bar of the Year, and to have been nominated for the Yorkshire Life Food & Drinks Awards. Being part of the Tyne Tees Television series 'Raw Chefs' gave us another opportunity to champion our region. Greens restaurant is open every evening and Friday, Saturday and Sunday lunchtime.

Rob Green, *restaurateur.*

GREENS

Lobster lobster lobster

Serves 2

INGREDIENTS

1 fresh boiled Whitby lobster, split in half, meat removed from body and claws, head sack removed, head and all shells reserved.

MOUSSE WITH SEAWEED:

300ml double cream

half the lobster meat, chopped

juice of 1/2 lemon

pinch cayenne pepper

1 sheet nori seaweed

LOBSTER SALAD:

other half of the lobster meat, chopped

1 tbs mayonnaise

1 tsp of fresh lime juice

4 washed little gem lettuce leaves

lime zest and paprika for garnish

LOBSTER BISQUE:

shells and head of the lobster

3 tbs olive oil

1/2 medium onion, finely chopped

1/2 celery stick, chopped

1 small garlic clove

1 lemongrass stem, chopped

pinch saffron strands

1 teaspoon Cognac

100ml Noilly Prat, or dry vermouth

1/2 litre fish stock

2 plum tomatoes

2 tsp tomato puree

1 basil sprig

1 tarragon sprig

1 parsley sprig

1 small bay leaf

50 ml double cream

METHOD

For the mousse with seaweed, whisk half the cream to stiff peaks, cover and chill for one hour. In a blender, blend the lobster meat for 30 seconds then add remaining cream, lemon juice and cayenne pepper until smooth. Place in a bowl, cover and chill for one hour, then carefully fold whisked cream into the lobster mix. Cover and return to the fridge for a further 30 minutes to set. Cut two diamond shapes 4-5 cm from the seaweed sheet, reserve. **For the lobster salad,** mix the lobster, mayonnaise and lime juice. Place this on two-fanned lettuce leaves and garnish with a little lime zest and pinch of paprika. **For the lobster bisque,** chop the lobster shells and head using a heavy knife – the finer you chop the more flavour you will extract. Heat half the olive oil in a large saucepan and sauté the head and shells for five minutes. Remove and set aside. Heat the remaining oil, add the vegetables, garlic and lemongrass and sauté for five minutes until softened. Sprinkle in saffron and cook for 30 seconds. Deglaze with the Cognac, add the noilly prat, bubble and reduce by half. Return the shells to the pan. Add the stock, tomatoes, tomato puree and herbs. Season with pepper to taste. Bring to the boil then simmer for 20 minutes . Strain the liquor through a large sieve into another pan, pressing the shells with a ladle to extract as much flavour as possible. Bring the strained liquor to the boil and simmer until reduced to about 300ml. Stir in the cream and simmer gently. Add salt to taste at this stage. **To serve,** pour the bisque into a suitable dish, on the centre of a rectangular plate. Place the lobster salad to the right and one seaweed diamond to the left. Using an ice cream scoop dipped in warm water make a round ball of mousse and place on top of the seaweed with the other diamond on top. Serve with warm bread rolls.

GREENS

13 Bridge Street, Whitby, North Yorkshire YO22 4BG
Tel: 01947 600284   www.greensofwhitby.com

GREENS

Fillets of Whitby brill with a ragout of queen scallops

Serves 4

900g brill fillets

227g queen scallops

100g button mushrooms, sliced

1 leek, thinly sliced

100g baby carrots

100g mange tout sliced

560ml fish stock

284ml Noilly prat or dry vermouth

284ml double cream

50g unsalted butter cut into cubes

Oil for frying

To prepare, reduce the fish stock by a third over a high heat. Add the Noilly prat and reduce by a third again. Add the cream, bring to the boil and set aside. Pre-heat a non stick pan with 2mm of oil over a medium heat. Season the fillets of brill and fry on both sides until just cooked, set aside. Sauté the mushrooms, leek, mange tout and carrots over a gentle heat until soft. Add the fish cream and simmer for five minutes. Stir in the butter, but do not allow to boil. Add the scallops and cook for 30 seconds only.

To serve, divide the ragout between four plates, place the brill fillets on top and any remaining sauce around the plate, garnish with a few crispy-fried leeks.

GREENS

13 Bridge Street, Whitby, North Yorkshire YO22 4BG
Tel: 01947 600284 www.greensofwhitby.com

GREENS

Trio of chocolate

Serves 4

INGREDIENTS

FONDANT:
100g unsalted butter
100g dark chocolate
2 eggs
4 egg yolks
100g plain flour
120g caster sugar

ICE CREAM:
300ml double cream
300ml milk
100g caster sugar
6 egg yolks
200g white chocolate grated

CHOCOLATE TART:
baked blind pastry case (9 inches round)
400g dark chocolate
150ml milk
250ml double cream
2 eggs, beaten

METHOD

For the fondant, melt the butter and chocolate in a bowl over a pan of hot water. Cool for 10 mins. Whisk eggs, egg yolks and sugar until pale, smooth and thick. Add the chocolate and butter mix to the eggs and mix well. Sift and fold in the flour. Place in buttered ramekins and bake in a hot oven, 230C, for 10-12 minutes.

For the ice cream, mix cream and milk together in a pan and bring to boil. Add the grated chocolate, Beat the egg yolks and sugar until pale and light, pour on to the milk and cream, stirring all the time until well blended. Once cool, churn in an ice cream machine until set, then place in a freezer.

For the chocolate tart, place chocolate in a bowl. Boil the milk and cream and pour over the chocolate and mix until smooth. Put the beaten eggs in another bowl and pour in the chocolate mixture, whisking well. Pour the mixture into the flan case and bake for 30 minutes on the lowest heat, until the tart is set.

To serve, place the fondant on a serving plate with a slice of chocolate tart next to it and a ball of ice cream in a small espresso cup, dusted with cocoa powder.

GREENS

13 Bridge Street, WHITBY, North Yorkshire YO22 4BG
Tel: 01947 600284   www.greensofwhitby.com

LA RIVIERA

LA RIVIERA

"Arrange a warm, cosy interior with buzzing ambience, add to it an extensive mouth-watering selection of continental dishes, place it in a romantic riverside location. Now parcel this with fine dining in a glamorous, relaxing environment and give everyone coming through the door the VIP treatment. Keep feeding this consistent commitment and dedication and you are on the road to success for years to come."

This is the recipe for success we have followed passionately since opening La Riviera in 1999. Our location, in a landmark building on the Gateshead side of the Swing Bridge is one of the ingredients. It is a superb setting with views over the Tyne and at night, by candlelight, is magical. We quickly attracted a broad and appreciative clientele. Our chef director, Will Brownlees, joined us two years ago and took our food to a new level. The menus he creates contain a mixture of Mediterranean and modern European dishes underpinned by the highest quality ingredients and presented with a dramatic, contemporary flourish. Will is a real showman.

Another key ingredient is the wonderful team I have acting as hosts to our guests. They set the tone of the evening and a welcoming smile and friendly attention are as important as the food and surroundings in ensuring they have a great evening. I'm very proud of them and of the high standards we maintain at La Riviera.

Parviz Alizadeh, managing director

LA RIVIERA

Fegatini chicken livers with bacon, shallots and sage

Serves 4

INGREDIENTS

300g chicken livers, washed	100ml red wine
100g mashed potatoes	4 chicken bouillon cubes
100g smoked bacon, cubed	60ml olive oil
4 shallots, diced	12 sage leaves
100g flour, for dusting	40g butter

METHOD

To prepare, place chicken livers in the flour and dust lightly. Heat a small frying pan with a knob of butter and a teaspoon of olive oil. Fry livers gently for 4-5 minutes, turning occasionally. Remove the livers from the pan and set aside. Add the shallots, smoked bacon and fresh sage to the pan. Sauté for 2-3 minutes, then add the red wine and a little chicken bouillon to taste and simmer for 3-4 minutes until the sauce has reduced. Return the chicken livers to the pan and simmer for a further 2-3 minutes.

To serve, arrange the chicken livers in the centre of the plate, place the heated mashed potato on top and drizzle the sauce around the plate. You can also, if you wish, top with puff pastry or serve on a crouton.

LA RIVIERA

Filleto al Riviera

Serves 4

INGREDIENTS

800g beef fillet steak, prepared

40g bacon, diced

4 potatoes, diced

4 shallots, diced

80ml red wine

beef stock cube, add to taste

60ml olive oil

40g butter

12 oyster mushrooms, sliced

4 rosemary sprigs

4 tsp tomato puree

METHOD

To prepare, pre-heat a frying pan add the butter and olive oil. Place the fillet of beef in the pan and fry on all sides for 5-6 minutes, take the fillet from the pan. Now add the mushrooms, shallots, potato and the bacon to the pan and sauté for 2-3 minutes. Add the rosemary and the tomato purée and stir. Pour the red wine into the pan and a little sprinkle of stock cube. Simmer for 3-4 minutes, adding a little boiling water if necessary. Place the beef back into the pan and simmer for a further 2-3 minutes.

To serve, arrange the beef in the centre of the plate and pour the sauce around. This dish is excellent with fresh buttered asparagus.

LA RIVIERA

Pipewellgate, Swing Bridge, Gateshead, NE8 2BJ
Tel: 0191 477 7070 www.lariviera.co.uk

LA RIVIERA

Panacotta

Serves 2

INGREDIENTS

100ml cream

25g sugar

5ml vanilla extract

1 cinnamon stick

10ml gelatine powder

METHOD

To prepare, place the entire ingredients in a pan and bring to the boil, stirring occasionally. Take pan off the heat and cool for 10-15 minutes. Pour the mixture into moulds and chill in the fridge for one hour to set. Once chilled, place on a plate and garnish to suit your taste.

To serve, surround with fresh strawberries or raspberries.

LA RIVIERA

Pipewellgate, Swing Bridge, Gateshead, NE8 2BJ
Tel: 0191 477 7070 www.lariviera.co.uk

LONGHIRST HALL

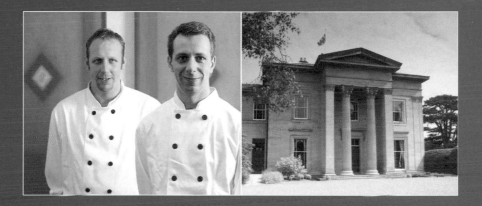

LONGHIRST HALL

Longhirst Hall, nestled in rural Northumberland, is set in 75 acres of woodland and landscaped gardens – a Georgian house designed by renowned architect John Dobson. Local chef Paul Harwood and his team have worked hard to establish the Boyson Restaurant as one of the best restaurants in the area, using the finest Northumberland produce.

Paul said: "This is my first Head Chef position, having gained experience working in a number of kitchens including those onboard the QE2, the famous Langan's brasserie and Harrods. Along with my Sous Chef Gavin Caldow we are fast developing a reputation for fantastic affordable food, winning a number of favourable reviews this year."

"Largely, we use local produce to construct a fresh seasonal *a la carte* menu four times a year, while our daily menu allows us to experiment and blend flavours to create some stunning dishes."

Deputy Manager Ian Paterson added: "It is particularly pleasing to see the same customers returning again and again and there can be no higher compliment than when a number of them have reserved a table for Sunday lunch for the entire year. The pianist, on every Sunday lunchtime and Friday and Saturday evenings, is the perfect accompaniment to any dish, allowing our guests to savour the atmosphere along with their meal."

Paul Harwood, head chef

LONGHIRST HALL

Pan fried scallops, black pudding, savoy cabbage, bacon and mustard dressing

Serves 4

INGREDIENTS

4 slices of black pudding

16 scallops, cleaned and roe removed

1 savoy cabbage

4 rashers of bacon

olive oil

DRESSING:

2 tbs white wine vinegar

1 tsp honey

1 tbs English mustard

10g sugar

olive oil

1 tbs lemon juice

METHOD

To prepare, heat frying pan with a tablespoon of olive oil; cook the black pudding for two minutes on each side, adding a little butter right at the end. Cut the cabbage into thin strips, blanch in boiling salted water. Slice the bacon into thin strips, fry and drain off juice.

For the scallops, drizzle a little olive oil in a hot pan. Sear the scallops quickly until golden brown on each side, then finish with butter and lemon juice.

For the dressing, mix mustard, sugar, lemon juice and honey then slowly add olive oil.

To serve, place the warm black pudding in the middle of the plate top with warm cabbage and bacon. Arrange the scallops around the edge of the plate. Drizzle the dressing over the scallops and garnish.

LONGHIRST HALL

Longhirst, Morpeth, Northumberland, NE61 3LL
Tel: 01670 791348 www.longhirst.co.uk

LONGHIRST HALL

Roast loin of middle white pork with vegetable ratatouille and cider fondant potatoes

Serves 4

1 loin of middle white pork
1 tbs vegetable oil
pinch of salt
pinch of pepper

1 aubergine, chopped
1 courgette, chopped
2 tomatoes, chopped
Fresh basil roughly chopped

RATATOUILLE:

1 of each red, green and yellow pepper, chopped
1 large onion diced into 1cm chunks
2 cloves of garlic

POTATOES:

8 large potatoes
1 pint cider
25g butter

METHOD

For the loin of pork, heat the oil and butter in a heavy cast iron roasting pan. Season the pork loin with salt and pepper. Add the loin of pork to the pan when it is sizzling hot, seal on all sides then roast in oven at 180C for 45 minutes. Remove and allow to rest.

For the ratatouille, heat oil in a shallow-sided saucepan, add onions and garlic and cook until just soft. Add peppers, courgette, aubergine and cook together for three or four minutes. Add chopped tomatoes, basil and salt and pepper and cook for a further three or four minutes, then remove from heat

For the potatoes, place the shaped potatoes in a shallow-sided oven dish about 5cm in depth. They should be placed in a single layer only. Pour over with cider until it covers half the potato, season and bring gently to the boil. Brush the surface of the potatoes with melted butter and bake in oven for 30 minutes at 170C. At regular intervals brush the potatoes with melted butter to prevent drying out

To serve, use a large shallow bowl and spoon the ratatouille into the middle of the bowl, placing slices of pork on top. Place potatoes at the side of the pork. Finish by pouring roast jus over pork.

LONGHIRST HALL

Longhirst, Morpeth, Northumberland, NE61 3LL
Tel: 01670 791348 www.longhirst.co.uk

Hot chocolate soup with black pepper ice cream

Serves 4

INGREDIENTS

100g butter	2 eggs separated
78g milk chocolate	3 tbs crème fraiche
40g cocoa powder	black pepper ice cream
100g caster sugar	(available from Beckleberrys)
2 tbs honey	chocolate soup

METHOD

To prepare, melt chocolate and butter together in a pan. In a small bowl mix cocoa powder, 50g caster sugar, honey, egg yolks and crème fraiche. Whisk the remaining 50g caster sugar and egg whites until stiff. Add melted chocolate and butter together with cocoa powder, caster sugar, honey, egg yolks and crème fraiche. Fold egg whites into chocolate mixture

To serve, place mixture into sugared ramekins, cook for 10 minutes at 180C, then serve with a scoop of black pepper ice cream in a brandy snap basket.

MANDALAY

MANDALAY

A taste of Asia is what we're about. An authentic and flavour-packed taste at that.
China, pan-Asia, call it what you will but freshness and fine ingredients are always at the forefront.
You might be tempted by dishes such as mussels with ginger and spring onion, seafood tempura with chilli and soya sauce dip, chicken with lemongrass and coriander or lobster with ginger and spring onion.
Inside the restaurant Feng Shui-influenced decor includes a contemporary waterfall and specially positioned mirrors. The contemporary lines of the interior design perfectly complements the simple dishes which make the most of great quality and fresh produce which works best with a fine balance of the most aromatic spices.
Our food is deliberately well thought out, resulting in dishes created with care.

Alex Shek, chef/proprietor

MANDALAY

Mongolian dry spiced chicken

Serves 2

INGREDIENTS

2 chicken breasts, sliced

$^1/_2$ large onion, sliced

1 spring onion, quartered

$^1/_2$ tsp crushed garlic

1 tsp curry powder

$^1/_2$ tsp chilli powder

pinch of salt

1 tsp vegetable oil

METHOD

To prepare, heat the wok, add oil and slowly cook the chicken. Add the onion, spring onion and garlic and stir fry until you can smell the aroma. Add the chilli, curry powder and seasoning and stir fry until they are infused.

MANDALAY

1-2 Holly Avenue West, Jesmond, Newcastle
Tel: 0191 281 8281   www.themandalay.co.uk

MANDALAY

Korean spicy beef

Serves 2

INGREDIENTS

400g fillet beef, sliced into strips

1 spring onion, finely sliced

$^{1}/_{2}$ large onion, diced

2 cloves garlic, crushed

1 tbs Korean hot chilli bean sauce

1 tbs sesame oil

1 tsp oyster sauce

2 pinches sesame seeds

$^{1}/_{2}$ tsp sugar

$^{1}/_{2}$ tea cup of chicken stock

1 tbs vegetable oil

METHOD

To prepare, preheat the wok to a high heat, add the vegetable oil and gently cook the beef until medium rare, then drain the oil from the pan. In a separate wok add the sesame oil and lightly stir-fry the onion, spring onion and garlic. Add the beef and chicken stock. Bring to the boil and add the chilli bean sauce, seasoning, oyster sauce and sugar, then let the flavours blend for a few minutes.

To serve, sprinkle with sesame seeds.

MANDALAY

Pan-fried king prawns

Serves 4

INGREDIENTS

16 butterfly king prawns (out of shell)

1 large egg, whisked

1 tbs potato starch

$^1/_2$ lemon, finely sliced, to garnish

1 tsp vegetable oil

pinch salt

$^1/_2$ cup lemon cordial

small piece pickled or fresh ginger, finely sliced

Juice of half a lemon

1 tsp sugar

$^1/_2$ cup of water

METHOD

To prepare, mix the lemon cordial, lemon juice, sugar and ginger together to make a sauce. Pre-heat the wok on a slow flame and add the oil. Mix salt and half the potato starch and dust the prawns lightly. Then dip the prawns in beaten egg and gently fry for a few minutes. Add some water to the potato starch to make a thickener. Add the sauce ingredients to the pan and cook, adding the starch mixture to thicken the sauce if necessary. Place the prawns on a plate and then cover with the sauce.

MANDALAY
1-2 Holly Avenue West, Jesmond, Newcastle
Tel : 0191 2818281 www.themandalay.co.uk

MATFEN HALL

MATFEN HALL

At an early age I was often present when my mother was cooking, always enthusiastic and excited to have a go myself. I first had contact with the commercial operation at fifteen when I became pot washer at a local pub/restaurant. This rekindled my childhood passions for cooking.

After finishing college I worked in London for a short time before returning to the North East. I have worked at Matfen Hall for six years, 18 months now as head chef.

Matfen Hall, being in the heart of rural Northumberland, has an abundance of fine local produce on the doorstep. All you need to do is look in the right places. Seasonality plays a great part in the writing of our contemporary English menu, although we do like to give it a continental twist.

I have learnt that a chef is only as good as the team he has behind him. It's all about coaxing the best from your team rather than demanding results. I like to involve every member of the kitchen team from menu development stage to the final dish. I give everyone the opportunity to put forward ideas.

This has brought the team together and produced a strong and versatile squad.

Phil Hall, head chef

MATFEN HALL

Crayfish risotto with Parmesan tuile

Serves 4

INGREDIENTS

RISOTTO:
200g crayfish tails (fresh or in brine)
250g arborio rice
500ml shell fish stock
2 shallots, finely chopped
1 plum tomato, skinned and diced
2 spring onions, sliced
50g grated fresh Parmesan cheese
75g garden peas

25ml olive oil
Salt and pepper

PARMESAN TUILES:
150g grated fresh Parmesan cheese

GARNISH:
8 mangetout
1 small jar black lumpfish roe

METHOD

For the risotto, heat the oil in a thick-bottomed pan. Add chopped shallots and sweat gently, adding the rice. Using a ladle add a small amount of stock to the rice. Stir continuously until all the stock is absorbed. Repeat for remainder of stock (10-15 minutes over medium heat). Add crayfish tails and spring onions. Stir gently and add garden peas and diced tomato. Add 50g Parmesan cheese to enrich the risotto, then season to taste.

For the Parmesan tuile, divide Parmesan cheese into four equal piles on an ovenproof tray. Grill until melted and golden brown. The tuiles are ready when cool and crisp.

To serve, arrange risotto on plate, top with shredded mangetoute, black lumpfish roe and Parmesan tuile.

MATFEN HALL

Thyme roasted partridge with morrel mushrooms and white truffle oil

Serves 4

INGREDIENTS

THYME ROAST PARTRIDGE:
4 oven-ready red leg partridge
1 large bunch of thyme
200g unsalted butter

ROAST ROOT VEGETABLES:
2 large parsnips
2 large carrots
1 medium swede

12 baby golden beetroot (red can be used)
100ml sunflower oil
50g unsalted butter

MORREL MUSHROOM SAUCE:
200g morel mushrooms
1lt game stock
200ml red wine
25ml white truffle oil

METHOD

For the thyme roast partridge, stuff each partridge with 50g of butter and a sprig of thyme. Season with salt and pepper. Oil lightly and seal in a hot oven proof dish on all sides. Place in pre-heated oven at 185C for 8-10 minutes. Remove and allow to rest for 2-3 minutes before serving.

For the sauce, heat the game stock and reduce by two thirds. Add red wine and reduce again by one half. Add the washed morel mushrooms. Simmer gently for 4-5 minutes. Season to taste

For the roasted vegetables, drop beetroot into pan of salted water and bring to boil. Simmer for 10-15 mins. Remove from heat and cool under running water. Tease skins from beetroot. Dice swede, carrots and parsnips. Blanch in boiling salted water for 2-3 minutes. Heat an oven proof dish and oil lightly toss the vegetables and add 50g of butter. Place in pre-heated oven at 185C for 10-15 minutes or until golden brown. Season to taste.

To serve, assemble the dish as required and drizzle with white truffle oil. Garnish with a sprig of dried thyme.

MATFEN HALL
Matfen, Northumberland, NE20 0RH
Tel: 01661 886500   www.matfenhall.com

MATFEN HALL

Pear, hazelnut and white Stilton crumble with red wine granita

Serves 4

PEARS:

4 medium pear	
200ml red wine	
100ml water	
100g sugar	
1 vanilla pod	

CRUMBLE TOPPING:

100g white Stilton	
100g rolled oats	
50g hazelnuts	
100g butter	
75g dark muscavado sugar	

For the pears, peel and core pears. In a saucepan bring red wine, water and sugar to boil. Split a vanilla pod down length and scrape out soft centre, add to pan. Add the outer pod for extra flavour. Add pears to cooking liquor and simmer for 10-15 minutes. Allow pears to cool in the liquor.

For the crumble topping, melt the butter in a thick-bottomed pan. Add rolled oats and brown gently. Break hazelnuts and add to pan. Add muscavado sugar and stir. Remove from heat. Break up white Stilton and stir through the mix.

For the granita, remove pears from the cooking liquor. Reduce the liquor by half. Remove the vanilla pod. Place cooking liquor into freezer. When liquor begins to freeze, stir to break any large ice crystals. Repeat the stirring process every 15-20 minutes until liquor is set almost solid. This will take about three hours. The liquor should have a slush-like consistency.

To serve, slice pairs and arrange in oven proof dish. Coat liberally with crumble topping mix. Place in heated oven at 180-200C for 10-12 minutes, or until the Stilton softens. Serve with lashings of granita.

MATFEN HALL

Matfen, Northumberland, NE20 0RH
Tel: 01661 886500 www.matfenhall.com

McCOY'S AT THE TONTINE

Cleveland

TONTINE INN.

—————

AT a Meeting held at the Town-House in STOCKTON, on the first day of February, 1804, in consequence of Public notice in the York and Newcastle Newspapers, and at adjournments the same place; and in YARM on the 16th, 20th and 29th month.

D I. That the sum of £.2500 be raised by a Subscription, in TONTINE, for purchasing Ground and erecting an Inn, on the new Road, from THIRSK to YARM, in the County of York, at or near to the Road, with the Road leading to STOKESLEY, &c. which will be from Thirsk, eight from Yarm, twelve from Stockton, eight from from Stokesley, and sixteen from Guisbrough; it being the that such an Inn will be of considerable public utility, and objects proposed by the new Road.

consist of not less than 50, nor m ous of forwarding the r es (not

MCCOY'S AT THE TONTINE

Sourcing the highest quality ingredients is always a priority in our kitchen. This is what makes our traditional meals so special, along with the cosy, informal and relaxed atmosphere here. The Tontine is an amazing old building, inviting, cosy and welcoming. It has real family history. The McCoys have, over the last 30 years, made this their home as well as one of the best restaurants in the area.

The menus are written by myself and David Pattison, an excellent number two in the kitchen and also another long serving member of staff, and comprise a mixture of influences including classic French, British bistro, Indian, Thai and Chinese.

I've been at the Tontine for the majority of my career. I started here ten years ago, leaving once or twice to gain valuable experience,but always returning ! It is a privilege to have worked with Tom and Eugene for so long.

Stuart Hawkins, head chef

MCCOY'S AT THE TONTINE

Seared scallops with slow-roasted tomato, Morteaux sausage, dill and red pepper dressing

Serves 4

INGREDIENTS

12 good size king scallops
8 slices Morteaux sausage
2 plum tomatoes
2 tsp pesto

DRESSING:

1 tbs cabernet sauvignon
red wine vinegar
1 tsp Dijion mustard
5 tbs olive oil
5 tbs chopped dill
1 red pepper roasted,
skinned and finely diced
pinch of salt and pepper

METHOD

To prepare, cut tomatoes in half lengthways, drop a half teaspoon pesto on each and gently roast for one hour at 120C. Mix the dressing together, adding the dill and red pepper last. Sear scallops and sausage together for about one minute on each side in a hot pan with just a little clarified butter and seasoning.

Gressingham duck breast with stir-fried pak choi and curried apple dressing

Serves 4

INGREDIENTS

4 duck breasts

2 confit duck legs

6 medium pak choi (blanched)

SPRING ROLL:

1 small carrot, grated

1 bunch of spring onions

1 tbs chopped coriander

confit duck meat

1 handful of beansprouts

1 tbs sweet chilli sauce

4 spring roll sheets

DUCK BREAST:

50ml sesame oil

50ml dark soy sauce

25ml toasted sesame seeds

1 inch root ginger

CURRIED APPLE DRESSING:

3 tbs lemon juice

1 clove of garlic crushed

120ml vegetable oil

60ml olive oil

1 tsp dijon

1 tsp curry powder

$^1/_2$ tsp grated root ginger

$^1/_2$ tsp hunssa paste

1 apple diced

METHOD

For the spring roll, mix all the ingredients together and roll in spring roll sheets.

For the duck breast, chop ginger and mix with liquids, pour over the duck breasts to marinade for two hours. Pan fry the duck breasts in a moderate pan, skin-side down for five minutes, turn and continue to cook for another four minutes. Remove from the heat and keep warm.

For the apple dressing, simply mix together.

McCOY'S AT THE TONTINE

The Cleveland Tontine, Northallerton, North Yorkshire, DL6 3JD
Tel: 01609 882671 www.mccoysatthetontine.co.uk

Glazed Lemon Tart with Lemon Syrup

Serves 4

INGREDIENTS

LEMON MIX:

16 eggs

700g Sugar

600ml Double Cream

6 lemons juiced and zested

PASTRY:

300g Butter (Soft)

500g Plain Flour

50g Sugar

3 eggs

LEMON SYRUP:

4 Lemons juiced and zest finely sliced

500g sugar

500ml water

1 tbsp Arrow Root

METHOD

For the tart, gently mix the eggs, sugar, cream lemon zest and juice until the sugar has dissolved. Leave to settle then remove any foam that appears. Blind bake the pastry in a 10 inch ring, then add the lemon mixture and cook at 150C for approx 30 minutes until the middle wobbles slightly. Remove from oven and cool completely.

Lemon Syrup, dissolve the sugar in the water and boil for 5 minutes, mix the arrow root with the lemon juice and zest then add to sugar syrup, keep stirring until thickened then remove from the heat and cool. To finish the lemon tart dust with icing sugar and colour with a blow torch.

OLDFIELDS

OLDFIELDS

At Oldfields Restaurants in Durham and Jesmond, Newcastle we believe we've created something a bit different in dining. Accessible is one word for it and a good one - because our aim is to bring great, local food to everyone.

We don't use the term "fine dining" in that our restaurants are anything but formal and stuffy. We want to celebrate the ambiance and conviviality of eating, just as is done in countries like Italy and France where excellent food is expected and so often delivered.

We also pay particular attention to the source of our food because we are aware that increasingly diners want to know where their meat, fish or vegetables have come from. It's called traceability and we make a bold statement about it with our 15 Mile Menu philosophy - aiming to source as much of our food as possible from within a small radius of our restaurants.

Local produce has always been a big part of what Oldfields is about and we're passionate about the North East, its eating and its food production.

There's a lot to shout about in our Region and at Oldfields we shout loud and proud.

Bill Oldfield, Owner

OLDFIELDS

Rosemary and citrus scented scallops

Serves 4

INGREDIENTS

FOR THE SCALLOPS:

6 king scallops washed and prepared

2 slices of day-old sunflower bread

zest of one lemon

zest of one lime

sprig of rosemary

1 tbs basil torn

butter 20g

1 tsp olive oil

FOR THE SAFFRON REDUCTION:

3 strands saffron

1 vanilla pod, seeded

a large glass of white wine

juice of 1 lemon

juice of 1 lime

25g butter

To garnish: 1 small leek finely shredded and deep fried (drain on kitchen paper)

METHOD

For the reduction, preheat a small saucepan, add the saffron, vanilla pod, white wine, lemon and lime juice and reduce by half. Then whisk in the butter and remove from heat.

For the scallops, in a food processor or blender blitz the bread, zest, basil and rosemary until you have achieved a green crumb. Roll the scallops in it until they are lightly coated. Preheat a shallow pan, melt the butter and add the olive oil (this will stop the butter colouring). Season the scallops and fry for one minute on one side. Turn them over and fry for a further one minute. Remove and rest on a piece of kitchen towel.

To serve, warm though the reduction and place one scallop on to a small dish then place this on to a larger plate, spoon the reduction over the single scallop and arrange the deep-fried leeks on top then place the other 2 scallops on either side of the central dish.

OLDFIELDS RESTAURANT

9 Osbourne Road, Jesmond, Newcastle, NE2 2AE
Tel: 0191 212 1210 www.oldfieldsrestaurants.com

OLDFIELDS

Northumberland fillet of beef, pancetta roast figs and blue cheese fondue

Serves 2

INGREDIENTS

2 fillets of Northumberland beef
olive oil
25g butter

FOR THE FIGS
2 large figs
2 slices pancetta

FOR THE FONDUE:
50g Stilton
20g sun-dried tomato
250ml crisp New Zealand chardonnay, such as Muddy Water

garlic
1 tbs thyme
1 tbs rosemary
2 shallots, finely diced

ROAST ON THE VINE TOMATOES
8 on the vine cherry tomatoes
1 clove garlic, finely chopped
1 tsp rosemary

PARSNIP CRISPS
1 parsnip, peeled, made into shavings with a potato peeler then deep fried until golden

METHOD

For the fondue, place the wine and sun dried tomato in a saucepan then bring to the boil. Turn down the heat, add the shallots, garlic, thyme and rosemary and allow to infuse for five minutes. Whisk in the Stilton and return to the heat to thicken for a minute. Remove from the heat.

For the steak, preheat an ovenproof shallow pan and add the butter and oil. Season the steak, seal both sides then place in a preheated oven at 220c and cook for five minutes. Allow to rest.

For the figs and tomatoes, trim the bottom of the figs and wrap in pancetta. Coat the tomatoes with the oil, rosemary and garlic and roast them in the oven for five minutes.

To serve, reheat the fondue, if necessary flash the beef in the oven. Place a fig and half the tomatoes on each plate, spoon on the fondue and place the beef on top.

OLDFIELDS RESTAURANT

9 Osbourne Road, Jesmond, Newcastle, NE2 2AE
Tel: 0191 212 1210 www.oldfieldsrestaurants.com

OLDFIELDS

Avocado and North Sea crab tian

Serves 2

INGREDIENTS

1 large crab

FOR THE TOMATOES

8 on the vine cherry tomatoes

1 tsp thyme, chopped

sea salt

1 clove garlic, chopped

FOR THE AVOCADO:

1 large ripe avocado

FOR THE RASPBERRY DRESSING

1 tbs cherry vinegar

3 tbs olive oil

1 tsp water

200g fresh raspberries

METHOD

For the crab, buy the crab fresh from the local fish supplier. Bring one litre of water to the boil and add 25g of salt. Boil the crab in the water for 15 minutes, remove from the pan. Allow to cool in a cold area of the kitchen. Once cold, break off the claws and remove the white and brown meat from the body shell. **For the tomatoes,** oil a small roasting tin and place in the tomatoes, season with the salt, garlic and thyme. Roast for five minutes at 220c, then allow to cool. **For the avocado,** cut the avocado in half and remove the stone. Peel and dice into small pieces.

For the dressing, place the cherry vinegar, olive oil, water and raspberries in a blender and blitz for 2 minutes. Pass through a fine sieve to remove the seeds.

To serve, put a metal ring on to serving dish and half fill with avocado. Then pile some crab meat, more avocado then top with crab meat. Press to ensure a compact mould, and top with a crab claw. Fill a small glass with the dressing, and serve.

OLDFIELDS RESTAURANT

9 Osbourne Road, Jesmond, Newcastle, NE2 2AE
Tel: 0191 212 1210 www.oldfieldsrestaurants.com

PARADISO

PARADISO

Located in an old city-centre printing works just off Pilgrim Street, Paradiso is one of the De Giorgi family's Gusto Group of companies. It combines a stylish mix of affordable yet outstanding Mediterranean eating with innovative design.

The menu is influenced by my total immersion in the Southern Mediterranean and North African food cultures. Having grown up in a family of traiteure owners in Tangier I continued my culinary education in some of the best hotels and restaurants of Southern Spain and Southern France until my heart ruled my head and I made Newcastle my home. The sun still shines every day as I work with my team dedicated to bringing the best of the Mediterranean heartland to my customers. A typical dish from my menu is given a unique twist, a uniquely authentic Moroccan tagine of Northumberland lamb is created with my handmade spice mix, which my mother still sends me. Dried prunes, cinnamon, toasted sesame seeds and fresh pomegranate complete this dish with homemade coriander flat bread fresh from our bakery. Upstairs you'll find me in the open plan kitchen creating dishes to warm even the coldest North East days.

Larbi Kamouni, executive chef

PARADISO

Grilled marinated local red mullet with chermoula and orange and beetroot salad

Serves 4

INGREDIENTS

4 large, fresh local red mullet	Juice 1 lemon
3 cloves garlic	1 cup olive oil
3 shallots	5 beetroots
3 large plum tomatoes	1 large Seville orange
1 tsp cumin	$1/2$ tsp crushed chilli
1 tsp paprika	1 tbs balsamic vinegar
1 bunch of coriander, chopped	

METHOD

To prepare, scale, gut and fillet the fish. For the marinade, mix two finely sliced cloves of garlic with $1/2$ a cup of olive oil, $1/2$ teaspoon of paprika, $1/2$ teaspoon of cumin, juice of $1/2$ a lemon and $1/2$ teaspoon of sea salt. Add the fillet of fish and marinade in the fridge for two hours. For the tomato chermoula, brown the finely chopped shallots in olive oil, add a finely chopped garlic clove, then the rest of the cumin, paprika and chilli. Add the diced, skinned, seeded tomatoes, season with salt and cook for eight minutes on a low heat, finish with fresh, chopped coriander.

For the beetroot salad, boil the beetroot until it is cooked, peel and dice into centimetre cubes. Finely chop the shallot, peel the orange, and take each segment and cut in half, add sea salt, balsamic vinegar and olive oil.

To serve, season the mullet fillets with salt and brush with olive oil. Grill one fillet per person under a hot grill for three minutes. Place the fish onto a bed of beetroot salad and drizzle the chermoula around the outside of the plate.

PARADISO

1 Market Lane, Newcastle, NE1 6QQ
Tel: 0191 221 1240 www.gustouk.co.uk

PARADISO

Moroccan lamb tagine with prunes and
sesame seeds

Serves 4

INGREDIENTS

1 leg of Black Face Northumbrian lamb, cut into 50g pieces	1 tbsp sugar
5 large white onions, chopped	3 cinnamon sticks
1 bunch flat leaf parsley, chopped	700g juicy, dry prunes
$^1/_2$ tbs turmeric	50g toasted sesame seeds
$^1/_2$ tbs ground ginger	1 tbs orange flower water
$^1/_2$ tbs black pepper	1 cup olive oil
5g saffron	1 cup ghee
	1 ltr water

METHOD

To prepare, in a large non-stick pan, or preferably an earthware tagine dish, mix the lamb pieces, 2$^1/_2$ chopped onions, chopped parsley, all the spices, olive oil and ghee and leave to marinate for one hour at room temperature. Over a medium heat, seal the meat until brown, add one litre of water and cook for 45 minutes. Then add the rest of the chopped onions and cook on a slow flame until the meat is tender, adding water as needed. In small pan mix sugar, orange flower water and $^1/_2$ cup water and cook until you get a syrup consistency. Add the prunes and simmer for one minute.

To serve, place five pieces of meat with sauce in a dish, or small tagine dish. Add six prunes, sprinkle with sesame seeds and serve with minted new potatoes and coriander bread.

PARADISO

Passionfruit and vanilla iced parfait with fresh watermelon

Serves 4

INGREDIENTS

200 ml water
300g caster sugar
10 egg yolks
4 egg whites
700ml double cream

50ml dark rum
1 fresh Madagascan vanilla pod
10 passionfruit
1 small watermelon

METHOD

To prepare, Grease a terrine mold with butter and then line with parchment paper. Heat water and caster sugar together until a syrup consistency. Add vanilla pod. Allow to cool a little then beat in egg yolks until frothy and light like a sabayon. Remove vanilla pod scraping seeds into mixture. Fold in cream. Whisk egg whites until stiff and peaking then fold into mixture. Add rum and passion fruit. Pour into a chilled terrine and wrap in a plastic wrap. Freeze for six hours.

To serve, Turn out and peel off the paper. Cut one inch slices. Put in coupe glass and add small scoops of watermelon.

PARADISO

1 Market Lane, Newcastle, NE1 6QQ
Tel: 0191 221 1240 www.gustouk.co.uk

PRICKLY PEAR

PRICKLY PEAR

Food, glorious food, one of life's great pleasures and one of the reasons why I took on the challenge of creating and establishing the Prickly Pear In Sunderland three years ago. Since then we have seen the restaurant go from strength to strength.
The whole essence of our being here is for people to simply unwind for a few hours, while enjoyong each other's company, the excellent wines, the exceptional food created by our talented head chef David Coulson, and also the friendly, efficient and unobtrusive service.
I think that we have brought a special something to Sunderland and the surrounding region, a rustic and contemporary retreat in which to relax and for once let life blissfully pass you by.

Dave Kilburn, owner

PRICKLY PEAR

Seared king scallops with Thai sweet chilli sauce, mango puree and frisee

Serves 4

INGREDIENTS

SCALLOPS:
12 king scallops
salt and pepper
squeeze of lemon juice
Knob of butter

SWEET CHILLI SAUCE:
3in piece of galangal
3in piece of ginger
6 red chillies
2 lemongrass sticks

4 lime leaves
50g fresh coriander
200g sugar
2 tbs Thai fish sauce

MANGO PUREE:
25ml white wine
1 mango

METHOD

To prepare, pat the scallops dry and remove the coral, season with Maldon sea salt and cracked black pepper. Heat a frying pan until very hot and sear the scallops for 30-40 seconds on each side, then bring off the heat add a squeeze of lemon and a knob of butter. **For the sweet chilli sauce,** blend together all the ingredients, except the sugar and coriander. Whilst the Thai paste is forming, make a caramel with the sugar by dissolving it in a hot pan until a light brown syrup is made. Add the Thai paste to the sugar and cook out for five minutes, then add the fresh coriander. **For the mango puree,** add the white wine and chopped mango to a blender and blitz to a smooth puree.

For the frisee, pick the yellow leaves and dress with cracked black pepper and Maldon sea salt and a splash of extra virgin olive oil.

To serve, space the scallops evenly on the plate and place a spoonful of mango puree between the scallops, add the frisee as desired and finish with a line of sweet chilli sauce along either side.

PRICKLY PEAR

4 Esplanade Mews, Sunderland, SR2 7BQ
Tel: 0191 564 0982

PRICKLY PEAR

Roast rump of Northumbrian lamb with
a rosemary and garlic mousse, turnip puree,
baby vegetables and roast jus.

Serves 4

INGREDIENTS

NORTHUMBERLAND LAMB:

4 Northumbrian lamb rumps
2 chicken breasts
1 egg
50g rosemary
50g thyme
50g chives
4 baby carrots
4 baby leeks
4 baby swede
1 turnip
6 desiree potatoes

RED WINE SAUCE:

750ml red wine
1 stick of celery
1 carrot
1 onion
4 cloves of garlic
1 bay leaf
1 thyme sprig
pinch sugar
500ml veal stock
25ml salted butter
sea salt and black pepper to season

METHOD

Method, firstly remove the excess fat from both the chicken breasts and the rumps of lamb. In a food processor blend the chives, rosemary, garlic and thyme, add the chicken breasts and blend for a further two minutes, then add the egg. On a flat work surface place three sheets of cling film on top of each other and paste an even depth square of your mousse onto this, put the lamb rump at the top of the square and wrap the mousse around the lamb, leave in the fridge for 30 minutes to set. Drop the lamb, still in the cling film, into a pan of boiling water for three minutes to set the chicken mousse. Remove from the water and take the cling film off. In a frying pan heat up some butter, salt and pepper, brown the lamb on all sides then place in the oven for six minutes remove from the pan and rest. **For the turnip puree,** peel and roughly chop the turnip and potatoes. Put them into a thick bottomed pan, cover with salted boiling water and cook for 15-20 minutes. When tender pass through a mouli and add reduced cream and butter. **For the baby vegetables,** peel and wash the vegetables then cook in boiling salted water for three minutes, remove and refresh in ice cold water. **For the sauce,** Simmer ingredients until sticky and syrupy, add the stock and simmer for a further 25-30 minutes. Strain into a clean pan and set aside keeping warm. **To serve,** heat the turnip puree up in a little butter, stirring constantly. Blanche the baby vegetables in boiling salted water, remove and add a knob of butter. Cut the lamb at an angle and place on top of the puree with vegetables.

PRICKLY PEAR

4 Esplanade Mews, Sunderland, SR2 7BQ
Tel: 0191 564 0982

PRICKLY PEAR

Poached Prickly Pear baklava with honey and vanilla ice cream

Serves 4

INGREDIENTS

4 pears	4 cloves
2 sheets filo pastry	750ml sweet dessert wine
250g walnuts	4 balls of vanilla ice cream
1 star anise	4 tablespoons of runny honey
1 cinnamon stick	25g butter

METHOD

For the baklava discs, lay the sheets of filo pastry on a clean dry surface, and paste liberally with butter, cut out the discs of pastry, eight large discs and eight smaller ones. On one sprinkle on top minced walnuts, ensuring an even coating and thickness. Now lay on top the other disc of filo, already buttered, on top of the walnuts, repeat this process with all the discs to form four large and four smaller. Put them onto a baking mat and tray and bake in the oven at 160C for three minutes. Remove from the oven and set aside.

For the poached pear, in a thick bottomed saucepan put 750ml of sweet dessert wine, the star anise, cloves and cinnamon stick, along with four peeled pears bring to the boil and simmer gently for six minutes, remove from the cooking liqueur.

To serve, slice the pears into three pieces and place the discs in between the pear pieces, put into the centre of the plate, place a ball of vanilla ice cream to the side and drizzle liberally with runny honey, garnish with spun sugar.

PRICKLY PEAR

4 Esplanade Mews, Sunderland, SR2 7BQ
Tel: 0191 564 0982

THE PUMPHOUSE

THE PUMPHOUSE

The Pumphouse opened in December 2002, specialising in seafood and steak with an imaginative, adventurous twist.

A popular restaurant set in an elegant restored Victorian waterworks, The Pumphouse opens for lunch and dinner daily, offering a truly unique setting bursting with genuine charm and atmosphere. With lunch menus changing weekly and dinner every two months, we aim to use the best of the season;s produce in a contemporary manner.

A typical lunch menu may offer slowly braised lamb shank with cannellini bean puree and thyme jus followed by our signature sticky toffee pudding.

I've been here at The Pumphouse for three years now and am proud to say that our emphasis on delivering excellence with outstanding levels of hospitality and service is demonstrated by the enthusiastic team of staff that I am fortunate to work with.

Having seen it develop over this time, I wait with anticipation to see where we can take it next.

Paul Beckwith, chef

THE PUMPHOUSE

Terrine of Scottish salmon stuffed with scallops and king prawns, wrapped in smoked salmon

Serves 6

INGREDIENTS

1kg Scottish salmon, skinless fillet
6 king prawns, peeled and de-veined
6 king scallops, roe removed
225ml whipping cream
3 egg whites
6 slices Scottish smoked salmon, thin sliced

selection of mixed leaves, e.g. radicchio, lollo rosso, endive
fresh lemon juice
salt and pepper
small handful of fresh dill
150ml light olive oil

METHOD

To prepare, generously double-line a terrine mould with cling-film and put to one side, making sure that there is sufficient cling film to cover the contents once the mould is full. Cut the salmon into large chunks and place in a food processor with the egg whites, blend until smooth then add the whipping cream and quickly mix. Add salt, pepper and lemon juice to taste. Lay the slices of smoked salmon in the mould carefully, taking care to overlap them slightly and ensuring you leave enough to cover the top once the mould is full. Spoon in some of the salmon and egg mix and smooth out. Place the scallops at intervals and cover with another layer of the salmon and egg mix.

Repeat the above step for the king prawns, using the rest of the mix to cover. Gently pull over the 'leaves' of the smoked salmon, again making sure they overlap slightly, then cover with the rest of the cling film. Place the mould into a bain marie and poach for 30-40 minutes at 210C until the terrine feels firm. Remove and allow the terrine to cool completely before removing the mould. **To make the dill oil,,** place a small handful of fresh dill into a food processor with 150ml light olive oil and blend until completely smooth.

To serve, in a bowl mix the selection of salad leaves with some of the dill oil, then place on the plate with a slice of the terrine, drizzle over a small amount of the dill oil just before serving.

PUMPHOUSE

Farm Road, Houghall, Durham, DH1 3PJ
Tel: 0191 386 9189 www.thepumphouserestaurant.co.uk

THE PUMPHOUSE

Marinated monkfish tails wrapped in Parma Ham, tian of Mediterranean vegetables with chorizo oil

Serves 4

12 small monkfish tails, skinned	4 small chorizo sausage
8 slices aubergine	salt and pepper
12 slices courgette	4 tsp turmeric
4 red peppers	4 tsp paprika
4 yellow peppers	4 tsp cayenne pepper
4 green peppers	large bunch fresh chives
12 asparagus tips	150ml vegetable oil
2 red onions	8 slices Parma ham

METHOD

To prepare, skin the monkfish tails, ensuring that the middle vein is removed. Using a pestle and mortar, blend 200ml of the oil with the chives, then transfer to a bowl with four of the monkfish tails, cover and chill for two hours. In another bowl mix the turmeric with 200ml of the oil, add another four monkfish tails, cover and chill for two hours. Repeat the same for the rest of the monkfish tails with the cayenne and paprika. Lay the slices of Parma ham onto a piece of cling-film, taking care to overlap them slightly. Remove the monkfish from the fridge and place each piece onto the Parma ham towards one edge. Using the cling-film to help, roll the monkfish in the Parma ham, forming a cylinder. Wrap tightly in cling-film and refrigerate for 20 minutes. **To make the tian,** slice the top and bottom from each of the peppers and discard, then cut the peppers into half. Blanch in boiling water with the courgette, red onion and aubergine. In a dariole mould, layer the aubergine, peppers and courgette, keeping the red onion in the middle. Place in the oven at 220C.

Warm a little oil in a pan, remove the clingfilm from the monkfish and sear on all sides, then place the fish in the oven to cook for a further 10 minutes. While the rest of the dish cooks peel the asparagus and cook until tender. Chop the chorizo into generous chunks and gently heat in a pan until it begins to colour. Drain the oil off and keep, discarding the pieces of chorizo.

To serve, Once the monkfish is cooked, set to one side while the dariole mould is turned out onto the serving plate along with the asparagus. Slice the monkfish and place alongside the vegetables. Carefully spoon over a little of the chorizo oil and serve.

PUMPHOUSE

Farm Road, Houghall, Durham, DH1 3PJ
Tel: 0191 386 9189 www.thepumphouserestaurant.co.uk

THE PUMPHOUSE

Strawberries and cream panacotta

Serves 8

INGREDIENTS

600ml semi-skimmed milk

1 vanilla pod

250g caster sugar

4 leaves gelatine, soaked

600ml whipping cream

25ml Grenadine

125ml hot water

Small punnet strawberries

Icing sugar

METHOD

To prepare, mix the Grenadine and hot water together with one of the sheets of gelatine. Halve enough of the strawberries to cover the bases of the dariole moulds, flat sides facing up. Once the jelly has cooled pour it over the strawberries, just so they are covered, allow to set. Boil together the milk. sugar and seeds from the vanilla pod. Add the rest of the gelatine, and stir until smooth, then leave to cool slightly. Whip the cream into soft peaks and fold into the vanilla mixture. Pour over the now set jelly, and place in the refrigerator to set. To make the coulis, use the rest of the strawberries, with just enough water to cover them and heat gently until the berries begin to soften. Blend until smooth and pass through a very fine sieve to remove all the seeds. Gradually add the icing sugar to taste.

To turn out the panacotta, dip the moulds into hot water and invert the mould onto a plate, pouring a little of the coulis round each one.

PUMPHOUSE

Farm Road, Houghall, Durham, DH1 3PJ
Tel: 0191 3869189   www.thepumphouserestaurant.co.uk

RAFFLES

RAFFLES

Set within a small boutique hotel on the outskirts of Darlington, Raffles restaurant certainly breaks all of the rules one expects from a hotel restaurant. The words chic, exotic and contemporary sum up what Raffles is all about. The upbeat, lively restaurant with handcrafted tables, 15 foot banana trees and colonial décor has a unique ambience. Hidden intimate corners, large circular tables and VIP section create the perfect setting for any occasion. The most appropriate way to describe the food is contemporary English cuisine. I joined the team just over 12 months ago and since then we have seen our menus and the restaurant's popularity go from strength to strength. Our food is deliberately contemporary English cuisine, the main philosophy behind this is to keep things simple, creating dishes with a combination of innovative flavour and textures, using highest quality produce from a wide range of local suppliers. Popular dishes on the menu include mini joint of James Wright gammon,egg and chips, and line caught sea bass with pancetta, creamed cabbage, champagne and mussels. The desserts also feed the imagination with our basil Infused bruleé and caramelised blood orange tart. At Raffles we strive to make every meal memorable.

Our surroundings do their bit to make this so and we hope the food speaks for itself too.

Mathew Robertson, general manager

RAFFLES

Home cured breasola with wild rocket and summer truffle oil

Serves 4*

INGREDIENTS

1 kg beef topside

MARINADE:

1 bottle red wine

500g coarse salt

20g salt petre or sel rose

200g brown sugar

2 tbs juniper berries, crushed

2 tbs black peppercorns

4 sprigs thyme

250g carrots, chopped

250g shallots or onions, chopped

250g leek, sliced

100g celery, chopped

12 red chillies, chopped

2 cinnamon sticks

GARNISH:

250g wild rocket

White truffle oil

25g pine kernels, toasted

Shavings of parmesan cheese

* 1kg of beef will make enough breasola for 12 people.

Garnish measurements here are for 4 people

METHOD

To prepare, bring the ingredients for the marinade to a boil in a large pan and leave to cool slightly. Place the joint of meat in a pot large enough to hold the meat and the marinade, then pour over the warm marinade. Leave this to marinate in the fridge for 4-5 days. When marinated, remove the meat from the liquid – the meat should feel firm and have taken on a dark colouring. Now the breasola needs to be hung for 1-1½ weeks, this can be done by wrapping it in a tea towel and tying it to a shelf in the refrigerator. This seems a long time to wait but it is well worth it! After hanging, when the meat is cut in half, it will have colours ranging from purple around the outside to bright red in the middle. The breasola is now cured and ready to eat.

To serve, slice the breasola as thinly as possible and arrange around a plate. Make a ball of rocket between your two hands and place in the centre of the plate. Sprinkle on the toasted pine kernels and the shaved parmesan. Generously dress the rocket and breasola with the truffle oil. For an extra touch, grind fresh black pepper over the meat to really bring out the flavour.

RAFFLES

The Croft, Croft on Tees, Darlington, DL2 2ST
Tel: 01325 720319, www.rafflesuk.com

RAFFLES

Gammon, egg, chips and pineapple

Serves 4

INGREDIENTS

GAMMON:

1¹/₂kg joint of raw gammon

500g fresh spinach

6 large chipping potatoes

12 quail eggs

2 pints light chicken stock

2 carrots, chopped

1 leek, chopped

4 celery sticks, chopped

1 onion, chopped

¹/₂ bulb of garlic, crushed

2 dsp coarse grain mustard

4 dsp clear honey

25g butter

PINEAPPLE CHUTNEY:

¹/₂ fresh pineapple, finely chopped

75g sultanas or currants

¹/₂ onion finely chopped

100g brown sugar

60ml white wine vinegar

1 tsp mixed spice

METHOD

For the chutney, combine all the ingredients in a pan, bring to the boil and simmer for half an hour or until reduced by half. Cool to serve. **For the gammon,** cut the gammon into four then tie these with three pieces of string to form mini joints (butcher's elastic can be used). Place the mini joints into a casserole pot along with the chicken stock, carrots, leeks, celery, onion and garlic. Bring to the boil on the stove then cover and simmer for 1¹/₂-2 hours or until the gammon is tender and almost falling to pieces. Remove the gammon joints then strain off 100ml of the cooking liquor to mix with the honey and mustard, this will glaze the gammon. The quails' eggs should be placed in boiling water for exactly two minutes then cooled very quickly in cold water. Peel carefully. **For the chips,** peel the potatoes and then cut them into even shapes – about 1cm by 8cm. Heat a deep fat fryer to 120C (this may be slightly lower than the setting on most household fryers). Cook the chips for approx 10 minutes until soft but without colour. Remove from the fat. Heat an oven to 180C and cook the gammon with a little glaze over each joint – this will take about 10-12 minutes. Melt the butter in a pan then add the spinach, season and then wilt the spinach for 2-3 minutes. Remove from the pan into cloth to squeeze out any excess liquid. Heat the fryer to 180C then fry the chips again for 3-4 minutes or until golden brown.

To serve, On a plate place four piles of the pineapple chutney around the edge, dress the spinach at the front centre and build the chips at the rear. Place the gammon joints on top of the spinach, spooning over any excess glaze. Now place the peeled quails eggs back into boiling water for exactly one minute more, remove and carefully trim the bottoms so that they can stand up. Remove the tops of the eggs to reveal the soft boiled yolk. Place these in between the piles of chutney. At the restaurant we finish the plate with balsamic vinegar and chervil sprigs, but these are optional.

RAFFLES

The Croft, Croft on Tees, Darlington, DL2 2ST
Tel: 01325 720319, www.rafflesuk.com

RAFFLES

Spring roll of poached rhubarb with grenadine syrup and ginger ice-cream

Serves 4

INGREDIENTS

500g rhubarb (preferably Yorkshire rhubarb, when in season)

8 spring roll papers (from Chinese supermarkets)

250ml grenadine syrup

125g sugar

100ml water

Ginger ice-cream, or vanilla with diced stem ginger

METHOD

To prepare, bring the grenadine, water and sugar to the boil and leave to simmer. Peel the rhubarb and cut into equal sized strips, about 10cm long. Place these, a few at a time, in the syrup mixture and poach for 3-5 minutes or until tender (do not overcook the rhubarb). Remove from the pan and cool. The syrup mixture can then be reduced by two thirds and cooled - this will be used to dress the plate. To make the spring rolls, make a paste of half flour and water then lay out the spring roll sheets. Brush the edges of the sheets with the paste and then place some of the rhubarb at the front edge. Roll this halfway down the sheet then fold in the sides, brush with more paste and then continue rolling to finish the spring roll. Repeat this with all the other spring rolls.

To serve, heat a deep fat fryer to 180C then fry the spring rolls for 3-4 minutes or until golden brown and crisp. Remove the spring rolls into a bowl with caster sugar and toss so that the rolls are covered with sugar. Dress the plate with a little of the syrup. Carve the ends of the spring rolls to remove any excess pastry, then carve one spring roll in half straight and the other at a steep angle. Sit one spring roll on the plate and stand the other angled spring roll either side. Finish with the ice-cream and serve.

RAFFLES

The Croft, Croft on Tees, Darlington, DL2 2ST
Tel: 01325 720319, www.rafflesuk.com

ROUÉ

I happen to be working here by pure chance! I was living in Guernsey with my wife and young daughters in spring 2004. My wife took it upon herself to enquire about a job as head chef at a new and exciting restaurant back in the North East. After speaking to owners, David and Helen, I know that I could not pass up this fantastic opportunity.

Roué is a stylish restaurant set in the heart of historic Hexham. In just six months the strong, dedicated team has already built itself quite a reputation. I feel lucky to have been here since day one.

Our philosophy is all about creating clean and uncomplicated food, perfectly delivered. It has been our traditional dishes like herb crusted rack of lamb with Madeira sauce which seem to have put us on the culinary map.

In such a short space of time we've created something very special, and now the focus is on our continued success.

Craig McMeeken, head chef

ROUÉ

Dressed Craster crab with Parmesan and sesame tuiles

Serves 4

CRAB:

250g white Craster crab meat

125ml crème fraiche

200ml mayonnaise

80g cucumber peeled and deseeded, cut into 5mm dice

4 plum tomatoes peeled and deseeded, cut into 1cm dice

1 tsp finely shredded flat leaf parsley

1 tsp finely shredded mint leaves

half a red chilli, deseeded & finely diced

TUILES:

40g grated Parmesan

2 tablespoons of sesame seeds

METHOD

For the crab, mix the white meat with one third of the mayonnaise and half of the crème fraiche. Check the seasoning at this stage. In a bowl carefully mix the cucumber, half of the diced tomatoes, the shredded mint and the finely diced chilli. Mix thoroughly and correct the seasoning. In a separate bowl, add the remaining mayonnaise, shredded parsley and some cracked black pepper. To assemble the dish, place a 7cm metal cutter in the centre of the plate and carefully spoon in the cucumber mix until approximately half full. Finish by carefully filling the cutter to the top with the crab meat. Spoon a little of the parsley mayonnaise around the cutter and arrange the remaining diced tomatoes around it. Remove the metal cutter and finish by garnishing with a Parmesan and sesame tuile.

For the tuile, place the grated Parmesan and sesame seeds onto a non stick mat and place on a baking tray. Place in a warm oven, 180C and simply allow the Parmesan to melt. Remove from the oven when the cheese begins to bubble and allow to cool and go crispy.

ROUÉ DINING ROOM AND LOUNGE

Gilesgate House, 4-6 Gilesgate, Hexham, Northumberland, NE46 3NJ
Tel: 01434 602110

ROUÉ

Braised belly pork with polenta cakes, glazed vegetables and sweet garlic

Serves 4

INGREDIENTS

900g Belly pork

Maldon sea salt

Cracked black pepper

POLENTA:

1lt chicken stock

1lt water

Half a teaspoon minced garlic

250g of polenta

100g unsalted butter

2 tbs mascarpone

1 tsp chopped chives

salt and pepper

2 tbs Dijon mustard

breadcrumbs

1 tsp unsalted butter

BRAISING LIQUID:

2 leeks, cut into inch pieces

4 carrots, cut into inch pieces

2 Spanish onions, cut into inch pieces

half a large head of garlic

1 bay leaf

4 sprigs thyme

3 tsp Italian parsley

2 lt chicken stock

1 lt beef stock

SAUCE:

100ml braising liquid

2 tbs diced shallots

1 tbs chopped parsley

VEGETABLE GARNISH:

10 turned carrots

10 batons celery

10 inch ovals turnip

12 balls beetroot

4 peeled garlic cloves

pinch sugar

1 tbs chopped chives

1 tbs olive oil

METHOD

For the meat, preheat the oven to 180C. Trim the bottom of the belly pork and season generously. In a large roasting tray heat the oil and carefully place the pork in skin side down. Sear until crisp and golden brown. Turn over and repeat. Remove the pork and discard any oil. Return the tray to the heat and add all vegetables and herbs, cooking until vegetables begin to caramelise. Return the meat, add the stocks and cover with foil. Bring to a gentle simmer on the stove before transferring to the oven for four hours. When ready, remove any bones and season thoroughly. Place a tray on top of the meat and press overnight. Pass the stock and refrigerate. **For the polenta,** bring chicken stock, water and garlic to the boil and whisk in the polenta. Be careful just to simmer as polenta will thicken very quickly. After about 10 minutes stir in the mascarpone, butter and chives. Spread on a large baking sheet and allow to cool. Par-boil the vegetables in salted water. Cook beetroot in a separate pan. Once blanched, refresh in iced cold water. Boil the garlic cloves until tender. **To serve,** cut the polenta, brush with mustard and roll in breadcrumbs. Gently sauté until warmed through and evenly coloured. Cut out the pork and reheat for 2-3 minutes. Melt the sugar and butter in a pan, once hot add garlic and sauté for 2-3 minutes. Remove the garlic and add the blanched vegetables and heat until evenly coloured, adding chopped chives. Place the polenta in the centre of the dish with pork above and finish by carefully arranging the vegetables on top. Warm the sauce in a small pan, stir in diced shallots and chopped parsley. Pour around the pork and vegetables to finish.

ROUÉ DINING ROOM AND LOUNGE

Gilesgate House, 4-6 Gilesgate, Hexham, Northumberland, NE46 3NJ
Tel: 01434 602110

ROUÉ

Pineapple fusion with spicy stock syrup

Serves 4

INGREDIENTS

ROASTED PINEAPPLE:

1 ripe pineapple

2 tbs spicy stock syrup

STOCK SYRUP:

2 vanilla pods

300g castor sugar

2 bananas, pureed

1 chilli, deseeded and chopped

20g root ginger, peeled and chopped

50ml dark rum

250ml water

PARFAIT:

8 egg yolks

250g castor sugar

300ml double cream

4 sprigs mint

50g fresh pineapple

METHOD

For the spicy stock syrup, remove seeds from vanilla pods, place seeds and all other ingredients in a thick bottomed pan and reduce until a syrup like consistency.

For the roasted pineapple, cut pineapple into 1cm thick slices and remove the core. Place pineapple in an ovenproof dish, pour half of the spicy stock syrup over the pineapple then bake in an oven at 190C for about 20 minutes.

For the pineapple wafer, reduce the temperature of the oven to 100C. Cut paper thin slices of pineapple, dip in the remaining stock syrup and place carefully on waxed paper and then onto a baking tray. Place in the oven until they have dried out and are golden in colour. This will take about two hours.

For the pineapple parfait, puree the pineapple in a blender. Boil sugar in a little water until you have a syrup like consistency. Whisk the egg yolks in a mixer until they become light and fluffy. While the eggs are still mixing, pour in the stock syrup and continue to mix until cooled. Transfer to a bowl and mix in the lightly whipped cream andpineapple puree. Pipe the mixture into a 7cm pastry cutter and freeze.

To serve, place a roasted pineapple ring onto centre of plate, drizzle with a little stock syrup. Turn out the frozen parfait and sit on top of the roasted pineapple. Finish by placing a pineapple wafer on top of the parfait, then garnish with a sprig of mint.

ROUÉ DINING ROOM AND LOUNGE

Gilesgate House, 4-6 Gilesgate, Hexham, Northumberland, NE46 3NJ
Tel: 01434 602110

THE STABLES

THE STABLES

Since leaving The Pumphouse, where I was executive chef and partner, 12 months ago I have taken over The Stables bar/lounge in Wynyard Village. Here I wanted to do something a little different. I didn't want to go down the 'gastro pub' route, I just wanted to create a menu that appealed to everyone, with influences from all kinds of food styles, English, Chinese, Indian, French and Italian.

My aim is to create something for everyone in an informal and relaxed atmosphere with good service and attention to detail, not to mention great value for money. Our two courses for £10 lunchtime menu is proving very popular, serving local quality ingredients at an affordable price. Also opening in 2006 is a heated patio area so customers can enjoy *al fresco* food all year round.

I hope to see you soon.

Marc Everson, chef/owner

THE STABLES

Pan fried king prawns with bean sprout salad and a chilli and soy broth

Serves 4

INGREDIENTS

12 large (6-8 size) king prawns

1 punnet of bean sprouts

1 red chilli, deseeded

10ml fish stock

1 tbs Thai fish sauce

1 tbs light soy sauce

1 stick of lemongrass

METHOD

To prepare, Pan fry the king prawns until golden then finish under a warm grill until cooked. Remove the prawns from the pan and keep hot. In the same pan add all the ingredients, except the fish stock, and cook for about one minute. Finally, add the fish stock and bring to the boil.

To serve, place a ring mould in the centre of your plate and fill with the bean sprouts, compressing them as you do it. Carefully place the prawns around a stick of lemongrass and pour in the sauce.

THE STABLES

The Granary, Wynyard Village, TS22 5QQ
Tel: 01740 644074

THE STABLES

Moroccan spiced lamb loin, goats cheese fondant, chorizo, sun blushed tomatoes and a balsamic reduction

Serves 4

INGREDIENTS

4 150g loins of lamb	4 tbs Morrocan spices
2 links of chorizo	100g butter
100g goats cheese	sprig of rosemary
4 tbs sun-blushed tomatoes	sprig of thyme
4 large potatoes	1 tbs of sea salt
284ml 10-year-old balsamic vinegar	salt

METHOD

To prepare, for the fondant, cut the potatoes into two round shapes and place in a pan with the butter and salt on low heat, until the bottom of the potatoes begin to fry and turn golden brown. Finish off in the oven until cooked.

For the chorizo, roast with the rosemary, thyme, sea salt and garlic in some warm oil. Reserve the oil that is left to dress the plate.

To serve, roll the lamb in the spices and pan fry until golden brown then roast at 200C for 10 minutes and leave the rest for five minutes. Place the fondant in the centre of the plate. Add a disk of goats cheese on top. Carve the lamb into four and place opposite each other, then place the chorizo with the sun-blushed tomatoes on top in between the lamb. To finish, drizzle with the chorizo and balsamic oil.

THE STABLES

The Granary, Wynyard Village, TS22 5QQ
Tel: 01740 644074

THE STABLES

Chocolate fudge brownie, with pistachio ice cream

Serves 16

INGREDIENTS

CHOCOLATE BROWNIE:

115g unsalted butter

300g caster sugar

1 vanilla pod

5 large eggs, lightly beaten

70g plain flour

230g dark chocolate, melted and cooled

70g cocoa powder

PISTACHIO ICE CREAM:

6 egg yolks

100g caster sugar

250ml whipping cream

100g pistachio nuts

pistachio flavouring to taste

METHOD

For the brownies, put the butter and sugar in a bowl and beat until soft and fluffy. Scrape the vanilla pod seeds and then beat in the eggs, a little at a time and sift the flour with the cocoa into the bowl and stir well. Mix in the melted chocolate, spoon the mixture into an a lined cake tin, spread evenly, bake in the oven at 120C for about 20 minutes until almost firm to touch.

For the ice cream, whisk yolks and sugar together until almost white, bring both creams and pistachio flavouring to the boil and remove from the heat. Then fold in sugar and egg yolk mix. Leave to cool. Churn in an ice cream machine for 30-40 minutes and then fold in the pistachios and chill for eight hours.

THE STABLES

The Granary, Wynyard Village, TS22 5QQ
Tel: 01740 644074

SEAHAM HALL

SEAHAM HALL

The renowned White Room, situated in the award winning Seaham Hall Hotel and set amongst stunning landscaped gardens on the edge of the North Sea, is a must for visitors to the North east.

The style of the White room is chic, with minimal deco yet comfortable surroundings.

The White Room's European specialities include; Roast Isle of Skye scallops with celeriac, truffle and lovage. Stuffed British pig's trotter. Morels, onions and sage. Venison saddle with pumpkin puree, seared scallop and chocolate sauce.

A fabulous cheese trolley combines the very best of local and European cheese, whilst the mouth watering desserts include passion fruit souffle, coconut sour and passion fruit sorbet.

The food is perfectly complemented by sharp service and the extensive wine list.

Stephen Smith, head chef

SEAHAM HALL

Roast sea scallops with celeriac and truffle, balsamic vinaigrette, apple jelly

Serves 4

INGREDIENTS

SCALLOPS:
12 sea scallops
15 slices of truffle
Maldon sea salt
$^1/_2$ lemon

CELERIAC PUREE:
150g celeriac
150ml milk
150ml double cream
5g celery salt

CELERIAC REMOULADE:
50g celeriac
10g truffle

2 tsp chopped chives
$^1/_2$ tsp mayonnaise

BALSAMIC VINAIGRETTE:
10ml 12-year-old balsamic vinegar
10ml truffle oil
10ml olive oil
5g chopped truffle

APPLE JELLY:
1 granny Smith apple
100ml apple juice
1g agar-agar
1g xanthium gum

METHOD

For the puree, place all ingredients into a saucepan, bring to the boil and simmer until the celeriac is completely soft. Drain the liquid but make sure it is reserved. Place the celeriac in a blender and blend till smooth, adding the reserved liquid if required. (You should be left with a completely smooth silky puree). **For the remoulade,** finely slice the celeriac into fine strips. Mix with the other ingredients, season and reserve. **For the apple jelly,** this will need to be completed the day before. Quarter the apple and remove the core. Chop and place the apple in the freezer. When completely frozen, place in a blender and blend with the apple juice. Pass through a sieve. Place into a pan and bring to the boil, add the agar-agar and xanthium gum. Bring back to the boil whisking continuously. Place into a container and reserve in the fridge. When set cut into 12 circles.

To serve, divide the celeriac remoulade between four equal size rings; place a slice of truffle on each one. Place into the middle of the your serving plates. Pan fry the scallops for one minute on each side, season with lemon juice and Maldon salt; place a slice of truffle on each scallop. Spoon three pools of celeriac puree around the remoulade and place a scallop on each one. Place a piece of apple jelly in between the scallops. Spoon the vinaigrette around and serve.

SEAHAM HALL
& THE SERENITY SPA

Lord Byrons Walk, Seaham, County Durham, SR7 7AD
Tel: 0191 516 1400 www.tomscompanies.com

SEAHAM HALL

Roast venison with seared scallop, chestnuts, pumpkin and chocolate

Serves 6

INGREDIENTS

6 120g venison loin steaks
6 scallops
1/2 lemon
Salt pepper
50g unsalted butter

GARNISH:
60g chestnuts
60g crosnes (Japanese artichokes)
100g pumpkin puree
1 lemon
1 small cabbage
50g pancetta
50g unsalted butter

CHOCOLATE SAUCE:
50g sliced shallots
50g sliced mushrooms
500ml red wine
250ml ruby port
1 lt veal stock
15g bitter chocolate
2 strips of orange
10 juniper berries crushed
25g unsalted butter

METHOD

To prepare, finely slice the cabbage and immerse in a pan of boiling water for one minute, refresh, in iced water. Fry the bacon in half the butter and add the cabbage, reserve. Reheat the pumpkin puree. Fry the chestnuts and crosnes until golden brown, reserve.

For the chocolate, caramelise the shallots in the butter, then add the mushrooms and caramelise. Add the red wine and port and reduce by two-thirds. Add the veal stock and reduce by two-thirds. Pass through a sieve. Add the chocolate, orange, and juniper and allow to infuse for 15 minutes. Pass through a sieve and reserve.

To finish, colour the venison steaks in a frying pan all over, and roast for four minutes (medium rare). Allow to rest for a further four minutes. Sear the scallops in a hot pan and deglaze with the lemon juice, season to taste.

To serve, place a pile of cabbage on one side of the plate and the pumpkin puree to the other, scatter the crosnes and chestnuts around. Slice and place the venison on the cabbage and the scallop on the pumpkin puree then spoon the sauce around.

SEAHAM HALL
& THE SERENITY SPA

Lord Byrons Walk, Seaham, County Durham, SR7 7AD
Tel: 0191 516 1400 www.tomscompanies.com

SEAHAM HALL

Deconstructed Black Forest gateau

Serves 4

INGREDIENTS

CHOCOLATE TERRINE:

sponge

4 egg yolks

4 egg whites

40g Valhrona cocoa powder

100g sugar

100g flour

CHOCOLATE MARQUISE:

75g single estate chocolate, 70   cocoa solids

15g butter

1 egg yolk

150g cream

1 egg white

15g sugar

CHERRY SOUP:

150 cherries

50ml water

50g sugar

METHOD

For the terrine, make a stiff sabayon with the eggs and half of the sugar, then add the cocoa powder. Whisk the remaining sugar and whites together until soft peaks. Continue both mixtures together. Fold in the flour. Place on a tray lined with silicon paper. Bake at 180C for 6-8 minutes.

For the marquise, melt the chocolate and butter together, add the egg yolks, fold in the cream. Make a meringue with the egg whites and sugar, fold both mixes together and put into piping bags. Place a layer of sponge in the terrine, then a layer of marquise. Repeat until the terrine mould is full. Allow to set, then slice.

For the soup, place all ingredients in a pan and bring to the boil. Pass through a sieve and reserve the liquid.

SEAHAM HALL
& THE SERENITY SPA

Lord Byrons Walk, Seaham, County Durham, SR7 7AD
Tel: 0191 516 1400   www.tomscompanies.com

SECCO

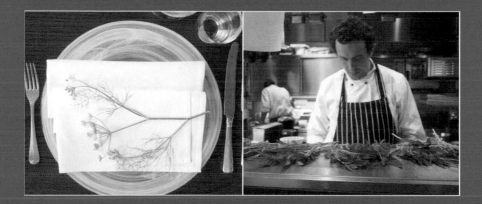

SECCO

Secco, winner of Harden's UK Remy award 2006, as "…surely one of the best Italians outside London", was born of a desire to showcase the combined talents of the De Giorgis as the pre-eminent restaurateurs of the region.

Elegant and opulent, the interior of Secco is designed to induce a sense of supreme well-being. It glows with rich colour, striking patterns and textured materials full of subtle detail. Joseph De Giorgi explains his love of the conviviality of food and drink as emerging from the culinary and social traditions of generations of Italian immigrants who made the North East their home. As a small boy the experience of making ricotta, bread and wine and collecting wild mushrooms from the Northumbrian countryside connected him to the possibilities of harmonising his Italian culinary culture with the abundance of local produce. Cooking his first meals in the family trattoria as an 11-year-old fuelled the passion that has inspired the food in Secco.

Sam Betts describes his journey into the unfamiliar and exciting territory of the Salentine Kitchen as a "revelation". Visiting Salento with Joseph, dining in restaurants, meeting producers and experiencing the flavours of the South has stimulated and excited his love of the culture of food.

Joseph De Giorgi, chef/proprietor, Sam Betts, head chef

SECCO

Involtini di carne con caciocavallo silano e prosciutto di langerano con fagioli stella

Rolled escalopes of local estate beef stuffed with cured ham and aged cheese, served with runner beans

Serves 1

INGREDIENTS

INVOLTINI:

2 x 100g beef escalopes per person (get your butcher to flatten some beef medallions into 5 inch diameter rounds)

25g baton of caciocavallo or peconno cheese

1 slice of good quality, sweet Italian prosciutto ham for each roll

1 fresh bay leaf per roll (involtini)

BEANS:

250g runner beans, stella variety or similar

3-4 mild chilli peppers, roasted and deseeded

50g pancetta

drizzle of Vincotto (see page 276)

METHOD

For the involtini, season the escalopes with salt and pepper. Place a slice of ham on each escalope and roll around a finger sized baton of cheese. Tie a bay leaf around the involtini with butchers' string. Place on a charcoal grill or grill pan and cook until cheese starts to ooze out of the ends.

For the beans, cut beans into small diamond shapes with single diagonal slices along the length of the bean. Cover the beans with salted water and two tablespoons of extra virgin olive oil. Cook the beans until tender. When water has evaporated, add roast chillies and cubes of pancetta and colour gently. Sauté all ingredients together and serve on a warmed plate with the involtini on top, drizzled with Vincotto

SECCO RISTORANTE SALENTINO

86, Pilgrim St, Newcastle, NE1 6SG
Tel: 0191 230 0444 www.seccouk.com

SECCO

Minchiareddi con ricotta stagionata al profumo di ginepro

Homemade durum wheat pasta with juniper smoked ewe's milk ricotta, courgette flowers, fresh oregano, and Puglian mandarin oil

Serves 4-6

INGREDIENTS

PASTA:

500g rimacinato durum wheat flour

1 tbs extra virgin olive oil

2 pinches sea salt

still mineral water to make elastic dough

SAUCE:

100g smoked ricotta, or any semi-firm aged ricotta cheese

1 tbsp of mandarin oil

2-3 courgette flowers per person

$^1/_2$ tsp fresh oregano flowers and leaves

1 small clove of garlic

$^1/_2$ small red chilli

splash of Puglian extra virgin olive oil

zest small mandarin

METHOD

For the pasta, mix flour, oil and water until a pliable but not too soft dough is created. Roll pasta into long 1cm wide rolls; flatten until 2 cm wide and $^3/_4$ mm thick. Cut into 3cm lengths. Place each strip onto a steel skewer and roll into an elongated tube 50 mm long with tapered ends. Place pasta onto fine mesh trays to dry for 12 hours. This allows gentle fermentation to take place improving flavour and texture. Bring a large pan of salted water to a rapid boil and cook pasta until *al dente*, approximately 6-8 minutes. For the sauce, cover the bottom of a large sauté pan with 2-3mm olive oil and heat until shimmering, but not smoking. Put in split chilli and a semi-crushed garlic clove and infuse until the clove turns golden brown. Remove both from the oil and discard. Fry courgette flowers after removing the bitter stamen. Cut cheese into matchstick-sized pieces and add to the courgettes after removing from the heat. Add herbs and zest and return to gentle heat. Add pasta directly from the boiling pan to the sauté pan with a little bit of the cooking water. Adjust seasoning, finish with fragrant mandarin oil and serve on a warmed plate.

SECCO RISTORANTE SALENTINO

86 Pilgrim St, Newcastle, NE1 6SG
Tel: 0191 230 0444 www.seccouk.com

SECCO

Mozzarelle di buffala "Inglese" con pomodorini e rucola

English water buffalo mozzarella with home grown wild rocket, oven dried baby plum tomatoes, gaeta olives and vincotto

Serves 1

INGREDIENTS

1 fresh 100g Buffalo mozzarella	De-stoned plump Gaeta Olives
Several leaves of intensely flavoured, locally grown rocket	Vincotto di "Gianni Calogiuri" (sweet wine dressing made from Salentine grapes)
Semi dried, sweet cherry plum tomatoes	Sea salt and ground black pepper

METHOD

To prepare, begin by drying the tomatoes. Pre heat oven to its lowest setting. Half tomatoes, remove and discard seeds. Place on a baking tray cutside up, sprinkle with sea salt and leave over night in the oven. Allow to cool completely and when still pliable store in sterilised glass jars under Puglian extra virgin olive oil. Store in a refrigerator.

To serve, Mix the ingredients and dress the dish with Vincotto di "Gianni Calogiuri" and black pepper The dish is simply an assembly of colourful, quality ingredients, feel free to be creative

* Plant wild rocket in the spring and pick the leaves well into the autumn, the longer you leave the plant, the more intense the flavour becomes

* English buffalo herds do exist and fresh cheese is available in small numbers. A number of companies provide temperature-controlled air freight of D.O.P. mozzarellas from Italy.

* Gaeta is a variety of olive similar to Kalamata.

SECCO RISTORANTE SALENTINO

86 Pilgrim St, Newcastle, NE1 6SG
Tel: 0191 230 0444 www.seccouk.com

SIDNEY'S RESTAURANT

SIDNEY'S RESTAURANT

Tynemouth village, with its interesting mix of bijou shops, affluent Georgian homes and long sandy beaches, really was the perfect place to set-up my first restaurant. Tynemouth is also a fantastic location for produce with the North Shields Fish Quay just down the road, providing us with some of the freshest fish and seafood around.

We even have the local divers bringing us ultra-fresh lobster, crabs and scallops so that the time from sea to the plate can be a matter of hours!

Steven McDonnell heads up our kitchen producing traditional, hearty and robust modern-British cooking using fresh, local and seasonal produce, often direct from small artisan producers and farms. Consequently, we are now just one of three restaurants in Tyne and Wear to be awarded a Michelin Bib Gourmand and, together with our sister restaurant, Blackfriars Restaurant in Newcastle, have an AA rosette and are included in the Good Food Guide.

Andy Hook, managing director

SIDNEY'S RESTAURANT

Pancetta and thyme risotto with Craster smoked haddock and a soft poached egg

Serves 4

INGREDIENTS

extra virgin olive oil

50g unsalted butter

4 garlic cloves, peeled and chopped

100g pancetta, diced

4 shallots, diced

3 sprigs thyme

200g arborio rice

175ml white wine

250ml fish stock, kept hot

dash of white wine vinegar

500ml full fat milk

1 fillet Craster-smoked haddock, trimmed

25g Parmesan cheese

4 farmhouse eggs

Maldon Sea Salt and freshly-ground black pepper

Chives

METHOD

To prepare, place a large saucepan on the heat with a small amount of butter and olive oil in. Once hot, sweat off the garlic, pancetta and shallots. Break off the small leaves of thyme and add them to the mixture. Once the ingredients are softened, add the rice and sweat off for one minute. Add the white wine and keep stirring the rice until the rice has absorbed three-quarters of the wine. Then add a ladle of stock and keep repeating and stirring vigorously until the rice has a small amount of stock remaining and the rice still has some *al dente* 'bite'. Remove from heat but keep warm. While doing this place two large pans on the heat – in one place the milk and in the other fill with water with a dash of vinegar. Bring both to the boil. Cut the haddock into four pieces and poach in the milk for about four minutes then remove from the heat. Put the risotto back on the heat and add the Parmesan and a knob of butter. Poach the egg in boiling water until soft (about three minutes) then remove from heat.

To serve, place the risotto into the centre of a warm bowl with the haddock and then the egg on top. Garnish with fresh chives and serve

SIDNEY'S RESTAURANT

3-5 Percy Park Road, Tynemouth, North Shields, NE30 4LZ
Tel: 0191 257 8500 www.sidneys.co.uk

SIDNEY'S RESTAURANT

Seared venison with puy lentils and bacon casserole

Serves 4

INGREDIENTS

50g unsalted butter

12 rashers of dry-cured,

smoked bacon, diced

2 onions, finely chopped

12 gloves garlic, crushed

4 sprigs thyme,

chopped plus more to garnish

4 sprigs rosemary, chopped

500ml red wine

300g puy lentils, soaked overnight in water

500ml beef stock

drizzle olive oil

4 portions of venison loin

METHOD

To prepare, heat a saucepan and melt most of the butter (retain a knob) in pan. Add onion, garlic, thyme, rosemary and bacon. Sweat off for a couple of minutes until soft. Add the red wine and reduce by three-quarters then add the drained puy lentils together with the stock. While this is cooking, add some olive oil and a knob of butter to a pan, add the venison and sear it until brown. Then place the meat under the grill until it is cooked to your liking. Leave it to rest for 15 minutes. Then go back to the casserole, taste and season. Make sure the lentils have absorbed the wine and stock.

To serve, spoon the lentil casserole equally into 4 warm bowls. Slice the venison on the angle to reveal the pink inside and lay on top. Garnish with some fresh sprigs of thyme.

SIDNEY'S RESTAURANT

3-5 Percy Park Road, Tynemouth, North Shields, NE30 4LZ
Tel: 0191 257 8500 www.sidneys.co.uk

SIDNEY'S RESTAURANT

Baileys bread and butter pudding

Serves 4

INGREDIENTS

25g good quality chocolate drops

425ml double cream

75ml Baileys Irish Cream

3 slices white bread, buttered

4 farm house eggs

50g caster sugar plus

a bit more for dusting

1 vanilla pod – seeds scraped

METHOD

Method, layer bread and chocolate drops either in one dish or four smaller dishes. Heat up the cream and Baileys in one pan. Whisk the egg, sugar and scraped vanilla from the pod in a bowl. Pour the warmed milk onto the egg mixture and whisk together thoroughly. Pass it through a fine strainer then pour over the bread, dust with sugar and then cook at 160C for 45-60 minutes.

To serve, simply serve hot with some extra cream if desired

SIDNEY'S RESTAURANT

3-5 Percy Park Road, Tynemouth, North Shields, NE30 4LZ
Tel: 0191 257 8500 www.sidneys.co.uk

THE SMITHS

THE SMITHS

Food is a family business, indeed, a passion for us.

We've invested a lot as a family in The Smiths over the past year and we are starting to see a real return as people come to eat here then return time and time again.

We've worked together in catering for a long time and when we saw The Smiths was up for sale we decided to go for it.

You get chefs going on about modern European and fusion cooking, but I'm not really into those sort of terms. What I do is take comforting, familiar food and present it well. I don't want to use lots of ingredients that are going to overwhelm customers. I want the food to be as relaxed as the atmosphere.

Our most popular starter is black pudding from an award-winning Scottish butcher, which I serve with filo pastry and caramelised apples in a scrumpy dressing.

One of the most popular main dishes is the roast rump of lamb with olive oil mash, honey and rosemary caramelised shallots in a red wine sauce. The lamb is from a butcher in Sedgefield who is excellent.

Barbara and Daniel Keen, owners

THE SMITHS

King scallops wrapped in pancetta with a filo pastry herb salad and a tomato, basil and garlic butter

Serves 4

INGREDIENTS

12 king scallops, prepared by your fishmonger	100ml clarified butter, unsalted
1 plum tomato, peeled and diced	80g herb salad
6 basil leaves, shredded	4 10cm square filo pastry sheets
12 strips pancetta	salt and pepper
1 garlic clove, finely diced	lemon juice
	olive oil

METHOD

To prepare, wrap the scallops in pancetta and leave to one side. Brush four small ramekins or espresso cups with a little clarified butter then lay a sheet of filo pastry over each one. Brush the outside of the pastry with more butter and bake in a pre-heated oven at 200C for about five minutes. Gently ease the browned pastry from the cups. Add the tomato, basil and garlic to the rest of the butter and gently warm through. Season the scallops with a little black pepper and cook in a hot pan with a little olive oil until the pancetta is cooked, about 3 minutes.

To serve, dress the salad with a little olive oil and lemon juice and place inside the pastry. Slice the scallops and arrange on top of the pastry and salad. Drizzle the warm butter over the scallops and serve.

THE SMITHS ARMS

Carlton Village, Stockton-On-Tees, TS21 1EA
Tel: 01740 630471 www.thesmithscarlton.co.uk

THE SMITHS

Roast loin of lamb, wild mushrooms and wilted spinach, potato cake and red wine sauce

Serves 4

INGREDIENTS

4 225g lamb loins

200g sautéd wild mushrooms

5 good handfuls of butter-wilted baby spinach

olive oil

900g potatoes, preferably desiree

100g melted butter

8oz red wine sauce

METHOD

To prepare, pre-heat an oven to 220C. Peel and thinly slice potatoes. Brush a small cake tin with butter. Place the sliced potatoes in a bowl, season with salt and pepper and mix in the rest of the melted butter. Arrange the potatoes neatly in the cake tin, making sure the slices overlap. Press down into the tin firmly and cover with foil.

Cook for approx 1¹/₂ hours, then ten minutes resting time, before removing from the tin. Take the foil off the tin about 30 minutes before the end of cooking time to brown the potatoes. Season and seal the lamb in a hot pan until nicely coloured on all sides then place in the oven, skin side down for eight-ten minutes depending how well done you like it. Let lamb rest for six-eight minutes in a warm place.

To serve, gently warm the mushrooms, spinach and red wine sauce. Place a piece of potato cake on each plate and divide the mushrooms and spinach between the plates. Slice the lamb and place on top of the mushrooms and spinach. Spoon over the red wine sauce.

THE SMITHS ARMS

Carlton Village, Stockton-On-Tees, TS21 1EA
Tel: 01740 630471 www.thesmithscarlton.co.uk

THE SMITHS

Summer pudding with blueberry and creme fraiche ice cream

Serves 4

INGREDIENTS

150ml water

130g caster sugar

850g mixed berries

3 tbs Creme de Cassis liqueur

6-9 slices stale white bread, crusts removed

4 scoops ice-cream to serve.

METHOD

To prepare, place the water and sugar in a large sauté pan over a low heat and dissolve the sugar. Add the berries and cook for six-eight minutes until they have softened, stir in the Creme de Cassis and turn off the heat. Line four timbale moulds with cling film, cut the bread into strips, dip one side in the juice then line the moulds with the dipped side facing the moulds.

Place the fruit in a sieve over the bowl to catch the remaining juices. Spoon the warm fruit into the moulds then press down lightly, cover the fruit with a disc of bread then with clingfilm, then cover each mould with a piece of cardboard and weigh down with some weights. Chill overnight.

To serve, reduce the remaining juice in a pan until it becomes syrupy. Turn out the puddings, spoon over the juice and serve with a scoop of good quality vanilla ice-cream and/or chilled creme fraiche.

THE SMITHS ARMS

Carlton Village, Stockton-On-Tees, TS21 1EA
Tel: 01740 630471 www.thesmithscarlton.co.uk

THE STAR INN

THE STAR INN

Born in Whitny and having lived and worked in and around the Esk Valley, North Yorkshire all my life, I've been influenced by all things local. From a farming family background, my northern roots have inspired my style of down to earth cooking. Taking old fashioned favourites and giving them a modern twist. Using seasonal produce from a network of professional and amateur suppliers alike, we have developed our much loved style of British cookery with Yorkshire influences.

One of only a handful of Michelin starred pubs in Britain, we have gained many other awards and accolades including three Cateys, the catering eqvivalent of the Oscars.

As well as The Star Inn, we've also developed other avenues of catering over the past ten years, with our self catering Black Eagle Cottage, Cross House Lodge accommodation, The Star at Scampston Cafe, Pern's of Helmsley Butchers and with our little Corner Shop Deli in Harome these have all been part of the building of our own foodie empire.

Andrew Pern, chef/proprietor

THE STAR INN

Elderberry wine poached hen egg with sweet onions, autumn truffles and hedgehog mushrooms, crispy Waberthwaite ham

Serves 2

INGREDIENTS

2 hen eggs

400ml elderberry wine or similar

2 tsp onion marmalade

Autumn truffle shavings (not essential)

10 medium hedgehog mushrooms (pied de mouton) or similar

a few fresh elderberries and sprigs of garden herbs for garnish

2 shallow-fried (approx 10cm x 1cm disc) flavoured white bread – garlic, onion or olive

2 thin slices of air-dried ham (Waberthwaite if possible)

50g unsalted butter

seasoning

METHOD

To prepare, warm the wine to a simmer, crack eggs into the pan, poach for approximately three minutes, depending on preference. Place the air-dried ham under the grill for two-three minutes to crisp. Warm the shallow-fried bread with a little spoon of onion marmalade on top under the grill, warming gently. Gently sauté the mushrooms in a little melted butter, season with salt and milled pepper. Check the eggs are cooked to your liking, remove and drain on a little kitchen paper. Place on top of the onion marmalade 'crouton'.

To serve, Place this onto a warmed plate, arrange the cooked mushrooms around the egg, sprinkle with a few elderberries, truffle shavings and garden herbs, place the crispy air-dried ham on top of the egg and serve immediately.

THE STAR INN

Harome, York, YO62 5JE
Tel: 01439 770397 www.thestaratharome.co.uk

THE STAR INN

Pot roast Duncombe Park partridge with Fadmoor beetroot, creamed curly kale, smoked bacon and thyme juices.

Serves 2

INGREDIENTS

2 partridge (grey or red-legged, depending on availability)

2 rashers of smoked bacon

2 turned barrel-shaped beetroot cooked in red wine with a little seasoning

8 baby onions

500g picked curly kale off the stalks

100g double cream

65g grated mature Lancashire cheese

200g creamed mashed potato with fresh thyme

10 cooked bacon lardons

300ml good game stock

1 tsp redcurrant jelly

pinch of fresh thyme leaves

METHOD

To prepare, cover the breasts of the bird with the bacon rashers and cook in the oven for 14 minutes. While the bird is cooking, reduce the stock. When syrupy, add the baby onions, bacon and beetroot and reheat gently. Warm the cream, when reduced by half, add cheese, curly kale and seasoning.

To serve, take the partridge out of the oven and rest in a warm place. Pipe the potato on to hot plates in a swirl, carve the bird onto the mash, spoon the creamed kale into a little pot or onto the plate with the beetroot alongside, sprinkle thyme leaves in the sauce, check seasoning, spoon over and serve

THE STAR INN

Harome, York, YO62 5JE
Tel: 01439 770397 www.thestaratharome.co.uk

THE STAR INN

Fresh lemon posset with boozy brambles and baked cats' tongues

Serves 6

INGREDIENTS

900ml double cream

250g caster sugar

juice of 3 lemons

30 brambles/blueberries

50ml Creme de Mûr or Cassis liqueur

caster sugar

mint sprigs

BAKED CATS' TONGUE:

30g unsalted butter

50g caster sugar

1 large free-range egg white, lightly beaten

1 drop vanilla extract

35g plain flour

METHOD

For the posset, boil the cream and the sugar together in a pan and cook for two-three minutes. Add the lemon juice and mix well. Leave to cool slightly, pour into cups and place in fridge to set. When ready to serve, warm the berries gently in the liqueur, place on top of the mousse with a few mint sprigs and the baked 'biscuits'. Serve on a saucer with a teaspoon.

For the baked cats' tongue, pre-heat oven to 160C, Gas 3. Line a baking sheet with non-stick baking parchment or a silicone cooking liner. Cream together the butter and sugar in a bowl until pale and fluffy. Gradually work in the egg whites, then the vanilla. Mix in the flour until just incorporated – don't over-work the mixture. Spoon the mixture into a piping bag fitted with a 1-1.5cm plain nozzle. Pipe 4-5cm lengths onto the lined baking sheet, spacing them apart to allow for spreading during baking. Bake for 10-12 minutes until golden brown at the edges but a pale golden in the middle. Leave on the baking sheet for a minute or so to firm up slightly, then lift onto a wire rack to cool and crisp.

These biscuits can be stored in an airtight container for a few days.

THE STAR INN

Harome, York, YO62 5JE
Tel: 01439 770397 www.thestaratharome.co.uk

THE TREEHOUSE

THE TREEHOUSE

Set in the heart of the secret kingdom of Northumbria the town of Alnwick is home to The Alnwick Garden, the most exciting contemporary garden to be developed in the last century. Here you will find The Treehouse, a unique setting for a restaurant, high up in the tree canopy. Inside the glow of candles and a welcoming log fire awaits, alongside a menu influenced by a fabulous abundance of quality local produce.

The Treehouse comfortably seats 100 and its design, using all things natural, creates a feeling of intimacy and comfort. Enjoy a drink on the exterior deck amongst the trees then take your place on an oxcart chair at a tree slice table for a fabulous meal with family and friends.

The Treehouse is open for dinner on Thursday, Friday and Saturday evenings and available for private hire Sunday through Wednesday evenings. The Treehouse serves a range of snacks and lunches throughout the day to visitors of The Alnwick Garden.

Richard Sim, executive chef

THE TREEHOUSE

Wild duck and scallop salad with burnt orange balsamic

Serves 4

INGREDIENTS

2 mallard ducks (or 4 teal)

8 large scallops, hand-dived for off the Northumbrian coast if possible

2 oranges, cut in half

60ml good quality balsamic vinegar, 8-10 years old

60ml extra virgin olive oil

mixture of baby salad leaves and edible flowers, washed

METHOD

To prepare, remove duck breasts from the birds and flash fry these in half the olive oil until medium rare, set aside in a warm place. Sear the scallops in the oil used to fry the duck breasts until crisp on the outside but rare in the middle. It is very important to colour the scallops. Set aside in a warm place. Place the orange halves flesh side down into a dry pan and heat until dark and caramelised. Squeeze the juice through a sieve and use to deglaze the frying pan used to cook the duck and scallops. Reduce by half. Whisk in balsamic vinegar and the remaining olive oil to make a dressing.

To serve, slice the duck, arrange with the scallops, baby leaves and flowers, pour over dressing and serve.

THE TREEHOUSE

*The Alnwick Garden, Denwick Lane,
Alnwick, Northumberland, NE66 1YU
Tel: 01665 511852 www.alnwickgarden.com*

THE TREEHOUSE

Braised shank of fallow venison in blackberry gin with buttered mash

Serves 4

INGREDIENTS

4 venison shanks
1 onion
1 carrot
2 sticks of celery
1 clove of garlic
1 sprig each, rosemary and thyme
1 bay leaf
1 pint good beef or game stock
1 large glass blackberry gin
50g butter

BUTTERED MASH

900g Yukon gold potatoes
1 egg yolk
100g butter
50g double cream
Salt and pepper

METHOD

To prepare, roughly chop the vegetables and place in a deep roasting tray with the venison shanks. Seal the shanks and vegetables over a high heat until the venison is golden brown. Add the herbs, garlic and blackberry gin, cover and place in the oven for three and a half hours at 150C. Remove shanks from the tray, pass the liquid through a sieve into a saucepan and reduce to sauce consistency. Whisk in butter.

For the mash, boil potatoes in their skins. Peel and mash the potatoes. Whisk in the butter and cream over heat. Remove and add the egg yolks. Serve with the shank and pour over the sauce.

THE TREEHOUSE

The Alnwick Garden, Denwick Lane,
Alnwick, Northumberland, NE66 1YU
Tel: 01665 511852 www.alnwickgarden.com

THE TREEHOUSE

Crumble of ginger roast greengages and nettle ice cream

Serves 4

INGREDIENTS

450g greengages or English plums

1 thumb-sized piece of ginger, finely diced

125g demerara sugar

75g plain flour

75g unsalted butter

ICE CREAM:

8 egg yolks

1 pint double cream

1 vanilla pod

2oz caster sugar

120ml nettle cordial

14g chopped fresh nettles

METHOD

For the crumble, de-stone the greengages and mix with 50g of sugar and the ginger. Place equally in four ramekins. Rub plain flour, demerara sugar and softened butter together until the mixture reaches breadcrumb consistency. Sprinkle the crumble mixture over the greengages and bake in the oven at 180C for 30 minutes.

For the ice cream, gently heat the double cream with the vanilla pod until the cream comes to boiling point. Take off the heat. Whisk together the egg yolks and caster sugar, pour over the hot cream and whisk in. Return the mixture to the pan and warm over a low heat until it starts to thicken. Do not boil. Whisk in the nettle cordial and fresh nettles. Place in an ice cream machine until frozen. Arrange and serve over the greengages.

THE TREEHOUSE

The Alnwick Garden, Denwick Lane,
Alnwick, Northumberland, NE66 1YU
Tel: 01665 511852   www.alnwickgarden.com

VUJON

VUJON

Vujon began life 16 years ago when the glamour and bustle of Newcastle's Quayside was barely noticeable behind rows of derelict warehouses. In those days it was quite something to set up here, but we like to think it was done with a daring vision which has helped promote the area as a place to find exceptional food and nightlife.

Our aim was to offer diners the very best traditional Indian cuisine in classical surroundings and consequently we have won ourselves a reputation as the best restaurant in the region for quality Indian food.

India has experienced many outside influences in its history, influences from a range of European settlers for instance, who left their mark on its culinary traditions. At Vujon you will experience these fascinating blends in dishes emanating from the Portuguese settled Goa or Kerala or the former French colony of Pondicherry, along with the finest examples of northern and southern Indian food. Our wine list has been similarly carefully chosen to provide the perfect accompaniment to your meal.

Matab Miah, proprietor

VUJON

Amm aur jinga ke sangam

Serves 4

INGREDIENTS

12 medium king prawns, slit and opened
$^1/_2$ tsp panch puron
from Asian food stores
1 tsp garlic paste
2 tsp ghee
2 fresh mangoes, peeled, to make 12
slices with remainder blended to a puree

30ml vegetable oil
pinch turmeric powder
water
pinch salt
$^1/_2$ cup rose water
1 tsp butter

METHOD

For the amm, heat the oil in a saucepan, add 1$^1/_2$ tsp garlic paste and pinch salt. Add the mango puree and thin with rose water. Stir and simmer it for 1$^1/_2$ mins. Set aside.

For the jinga, poach the king prawns in water with turmeric powder and salt for 2 minutes then drain the prawns.

For the ke sangam, melt the ghee and butter in a frying pan, add the panch puron along with garlic paste and a generous pinch of salt. Stir fry the king prawns for about a minute.

Serve with the fresh mango slices

VUJON

29 Queen Street, Quayside, Newcastle, NE1 3UG
Tel: 0191 221 0601 www.vujon.com

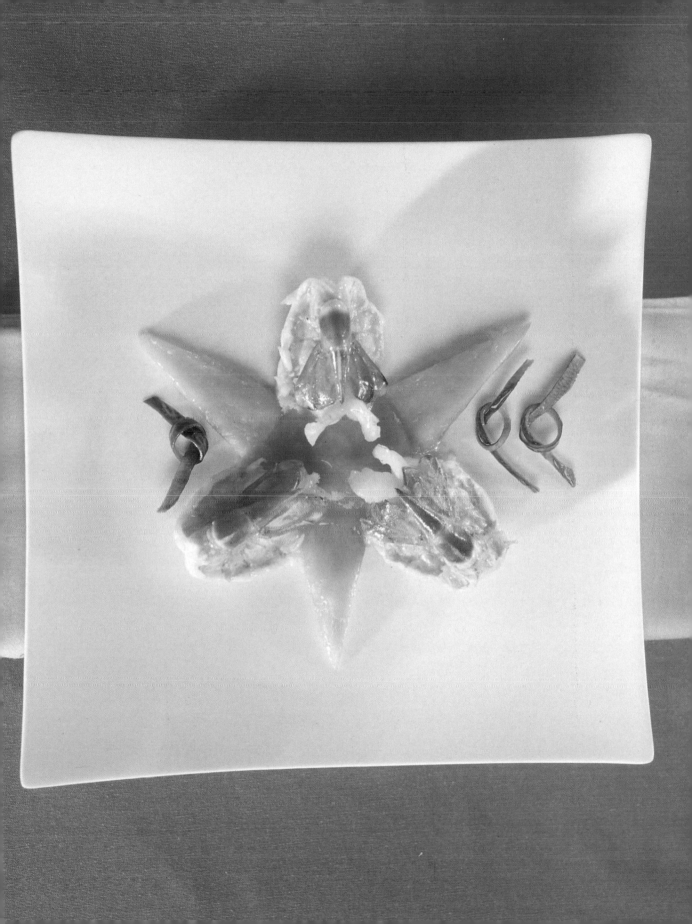

VUJON

Sas ni machi

Serves 4

INGREDIENTS

150g baby spinach, washed

1 medium aubergine, sliced into four rounds

130g tuna chunks

$1/2$ cup plain flour

vegetable oil

2 tsp pure ghee

1 tsp butter

4 medium potatoes, boiled and mashed

1 tsp yellow and brown mustard paste

$1/2$ tsp whole mustard

$1/2$ onion, finely chopped

1 tsp turmeric powder

$1/2$ tsp coriander powder

pinch whole cumin

1 tsp salt

4 tsp olive oil

$1/2$ tsp ground ginger

2 cloves garlic, crushed

METHOD

To prepare, melt the ghee in a deep frying pan and add whole mustard, garlic, salt, mustard pastes and butter. Reduce the heat and stir, add the mashed potatoes and mix. Cook for about a minute and leave to cool.

Sieve the flour into a mixing bowl together with $1/2$ tsp turmeric powder, a touch of ginger paste and a pinch of salt. Add sufficient cold water to form a batter with the consistency of double cream. Dip the aubergine in the batter and deep fry in hot oil until golden then drain and set aside.

Take the spinach and chop coarsely, then heat 3 tsp oil in a frying pan and add the whole cumin, garlic and onions and fry for about 30 seconds. Add the turmeric and coriander powder with a generous pinch of salt and stir for about 10 seconds. Add the spinach and stir. Once the spinach starts to wilt, add the tuna chunks and cook for another minute with oan covered.

To serve, make four flat rounds with the mash then the spinach and the aubergine. Make a tower with the rounds and garnish with sprigs of spinach and a drizzle of oil.

VUJON

Jallebi

Serves 4

INGREDIENTS

350g plain flour

cold water

150ml yoghurt

25g dried yeast

450g sugar

1 pint water

pinch saffron

6 cardamon pods

6 cloves

vegetable oil

METHOD

To prepare, sieve the flour into a bowl, add yoghurt, yeast and enough cold water to form a batter the consistency of double cream. Cover it and keep it in a warm place for about four hours to ferment. Prepare the syrup by dissolving the sugar in the water in a saucepan, together with the saffron, cardamon and cloves. Bring to the boil and evaporate until it becomes a heavy, thick syrup.

Take a medium deep frying pan and fill with oil. Heat to nearly boiling. Take the batter and using either an icing bag or a narrow funnel allow the batter to run into shapes resembling double circle whirls. Cook for about a minute, turning constantly until the jallebi is light brown in colour.

Remove, drain and immerse in the syrup for approximately five minutes, so that the syrup runs through the pipes of the jallebi without making the crisp outside soggy. Remove from the syrup, drain and garnish with icing sugar

LARDER

BAKERS AND CONFECTIONERS

Burtree House Farm
Burtree Lane
Darlington
DL3 0UY
Tel No: 01325 463521
Fax No: 01325 356608
E-Mail: enquiries@burtreehousefarm.co.uk
Website: burtreehousefarm.co.uk
Contact: Robert or Lea Darling
Produce: Award winning sauces, traditional and deluxe Christmas puddings, Sticky Toffee, Chocolate, Ginger, Toffee, and Pecan Puddings made with organic butter & cream. Gluten free Sticky Toffee Puddings. Tea Loaves - 13 different varieties including non fat and gluten free. Free range Chickens, Guinea Fowl and Kelly Bronze Turkeys slowly reared - no drugs or GM fed.

Donkins the Bakers
16 High Market
Ashington
Northumberland
NE63 8PD
Tel No: 01670 812126
Fax No: 01670 810736
E-Mail: chrisdnkn@aol.com
Contact: Chris or Julia Donkin
Produce: Bakery products.

Elizabeth's
13 Fair View
Prudhoe
Northumberland
NE42 6EU
Tel No: 01661 835515
E-mail: f.miles@btinternet.com
Contact: Rona Miles
Produce: Homemade bakery products. Sugar free cakes, Gluten free cakes, Wheat free cakes.

FM Foods
Unit 5D
Southwick Industrial Estate
North Hylton Road
Sunderland
SR5 3TX
Tel No: 0191 5480050
Fax No: 0191 5169946
E-Mail: info@fmfoods.co.uk
Website: www.tropicalwholefoods.co.uk
Contact: Karen Hetherington
Produce: Importer of Fair Trade dried fruits and manufacturers of snack bars.

Heatherslaw Bakery
Cornhill on Tweed
Northumberland
TD12 4TJ
Tel No: 01890 820208
Fax No: 01890 820208
E-Mail: info@heatherslawbakery.fsbusiness.co.uk
Website: www.ford-and-etal.co.uk
Contact: Colin Smurthwaite
Produce: Cakes and biscuits

Heatherslaw Corn Mill
Ford & Etal Estates
Ford
Northumberland
TD15 2QA
Tel No: 01890 820488/01890 820388
Fax No: 01890 820384
E-Mail: miller@heatherslaw.org.uk or tourism@ford-and-etal.co.uk
Website: www.ford-and-etal.co.uk
Contact: Julia Nolan/Elspeth Gilliland
Produce: Wholemeal, Rye, barley flour, Muesli, oat flakes, oatmeal, oat bran, toasted barley flakes, pearl barley, wheat germ.

Jenkins and Hustwit Ltd
Farmhouse Fruit Cakes
3B Laurel Way
Bishop Auckland
Co. Durham
DL14 7NF
Tel No: 01388 605005
Fax No: 01388 605005
E-Mail: enquiries@jenkinsandhustwit.com
Website: www.jenkinsandhustwit.com
Contact: Hilary Jenkins or Anne Hustwit
Produce: Luxury Traditional Fruit Cakes, Teatime Favourites, Dietary Specialities, and Christmas Puddings.

Loopy Lisa
A wide variety of home-made fudges and sweets. Fudge: Vanilla, Chocolate, After Dinner, Chocolate Orange, Milky Bar, Rum & Raisn, Honey & Ginger, Orange, Lemon & Lime, Coffee & Walnut, Black Forest, Cherry, Special Christmas Fudge.
Also toffee-apples, marshmallows, coconut ice, nougat, marzipan fancies including stuffed dates and stuffed walnuts.
Available from Barnard Castle & Stanhope Farmers' Markets; The Little Shop, Barnard Castle; JR Blackett & Son, Butterknowle & Woodland. Award winning fudges: 2005 Great Tastes Awards (Guild of Fine Food Retailers) Vanilla Fudge (Gold); Treacle Fudge (Gold)
Contact: Lisa Hodgson
Tel: 01388 718794 mob 07769 664944
Email: loopylisasfudge@hotmail.com

Mrs P's Country Kitchen Ltd
Unit 2A
Stainton Grove Industrial Estate
Barnard Castle
Co Durham
DL12 8UJ
Tel No: 01833 695508
E-Mail: enid4@btinternet.com
Contact: Enid Pilcher
Produce: Traditional style cakes, pastries and rich fruit cakes. Handmade loaf cakes, biscuits and cookies.

Nichol & Laidlow Ltd
Bridge End Bakery
Bridge End Industrial Estate
Hexham
Northumberland
NE46 4DQ
Tel No: 01434 600111
Fax No: 01434 600979
E-Mail: stephen@nicholandlaidlow.co.uk
Website: www.nicholandlaidlow.co.uk
Contact: Stephen Laidlow or Louise Thomson
Produce: Individual and Multi Pack Cakes, Tray Bakes, Muffins, Brownies, Flapjacks, Country Cakes. Bespoke and product development.

North Country Lass
11b Oakway Court
Meadowfield Industrial Estate
Meadowfield
Co. Durham
DH7 8XD
Tel No: 0191 378 0838
Fax No: 0191 378 9829
E-Mail: northcountrylass@btconnect.com
Contact: Ian & Margaret Grainger
Produce: Game Pies & Gateaux's

Northumbria Fudgery
2 Hallimond Road
Escomb
Bishop Auckland
Co. Durham
DL14 7SS
Tel No: 01388 664003
E-Mail: hallimond@escomb.fslife.co.uk
Contact: L. McRae or L.C. Readman
Produce: Quality fudge, 42 flavours including vanilla, chocolate, maple and walnut, rum and raisin.

Proof of the Pudding

Heckley High House
Alnwick
Northumberland
NF66 2l Q
Tel No: 01665 602505
Fax No: 01665 606945
E-Mail: rlgreen@heckley.fsbusiness.co.uk
Contact: Susan Green
Produce: Chocolate puddings, sticky toffee puddings sticky ginger puddings and dessert sauces.

Thomson's Bakery

385 Stamfordham Road
Westerhope Village
Newcastle upon Tyne
NE5 5HA
Tel No: 0191 2869375
Fax No: 0191 2869381
E-Mail: janian@geordiebakers.co.uk
Website: www.geordiebakers.co.uk
Contact: Ian & Jan Thomson
Produce: A family run bakery since 1956. A speciality bread range with the flagship Newcastle Brown Ale bread. Morning goods including bread buns, flatties and scones. Meat pies, pasties, sausage rolls, biscuits, cakes, tray bakes, fresh cream cakes. Sandwiches and wraps. Celebration & Wedding cakes. Christmas cakes, puddings (including Brown Ale), sweet mince pies, stollen.

Tyne Valley Fudge

8 Mount Pleasant
Stocksfield
Northumberland
NE43 7LP
Tel No: 01661 844294
E-Mail: amacklam@yahoo.co.uk
Contact: Angela Macklam
Produce: Homemade luxury fudges made with handmade jersey farm butter. Various flavours. Supply to Farmers markets at Hexham, Kelso, Berwick and Rothbury. Also supply retail outlets

Beverages

Pumphrey's Coffee Ltd

Bridge Street
Blaydon
Tyne and Wear
Tel No: 0191 4144510
Fax No: 0191 4990526
E-Mail: sales@pumphreys-coffee.co.uk
Website: pumphreys-coffee.co.uk
Contact: Stuart Archer
Produce: Freshly roasted coffee and locally blended tea.
Coffee machines and services available.

Redburn Brewery

Redburn
Bardon Mill
Northumberland
NE47 7EA
Tel No: 01434 344656
Fax No: 01434 344656
E-Mail: redburnbrewery@btinternet.com
Website: www.redburnbrewery.co.uk
Contact: Charles and Christine Sandford
Produce: Bottle conditioned and Cask conditioned Real Ale. Bottled and Draught Beer

Seaton Spring Water Ltd

The Waterworks
Seaton
Seaham
Co. Durham
SR7 0NF
Tel No: 0191 5131234
Tel Sales: 0800 0964 564
Fax No: 0191 5130600
E-Mail: info@seatonspring.co.uk
Website: www.seatonspring.co.uk
Contact: Andy Grantham
Produce: Pure Rock Filtered Water.

Thorncroft Ltd

Durham Lane Industrial Park
Eaglescliffe
Stockton
Teesside
TS16 0RB
Tel: 01642 791792
Fax: 01642 791793
E-Mail: enquiries@thorncroftdrinks.co.uk
Website: www.thorncroftdrinks.co.uk
Contact: Sheila and Guy Woodall
Produce: Specialise in making cordials mostly from old recipes and often using fresh natural ingredients gathered from the wild, or from our own organic plantations. We make five traditional and four well-being cordials, and three sparkling drinks.

Dairy Produce and Eggs

Acorn Dairy

Garhorne Farm
Archdeacon Newton
Darlington
Co. Durham
DL2 2YB
Tel No: 01325 466999
Fax No 01325 464567
E-Mail: organic@acorndairy.co.uk
Website: www.acorndairy.co.uk
Contact: Gordon or Graham Tweddle
Produce: Organic dairy produce including milk, cream, yoghurt, cheese eggs & butter. Organic bread, cereals, & fruit juices. Mineral waters (full range of sizes & flavours)

Archer's Ice Cream

New Moor Farm
Walworth Gate
Darlington
Co Durham
DL2 2UD
Tel No: 01325 300336
E-Mail: susan@archer7432.freeserve.co.uk
Website: www.archersjerseyicecream.com
Contact: Susan Archer
Produce: Jersey milk ice cream

Artisan Foods

Cowen Road
Blaydon
Tyne and Wear
NE21 5TW
Tel No: 0191 4141180
Fax No: 0191 4146680
E-Mail: sales@beckleberrys.co.uk
Website: www.beckleberrys.co.uk
Contact: Ian and Peter Craig
Produce: Artisan Foods are manufactures of Beckleberry's fresh cream ice creams and Artisan had made patisserie. We work from first principles to ensure superior quality products and offer a bespoke product service for larger customers. In the last 3 years we have won 17 Great Taste Awards including 3 gold awards and Best Speciality product from Northumbria.

Doddington Dairy Ltd.

North Doddington Farm
Wooler
Northumberland
NE71 6AN
Tel No: 01668 283010
Fax No: 01668 283033
E-Mail: enquiries@doddingtondairy.co.uk
Website: www.doddingtondairy.co.uk
Contact: Jackie and Neill Maxwell
Produce: Award winning luxury farm made ice creams, traditional mature cheeses from their own unpasteurised cow's milk; Doddington, Cuddy's Cave, Berwick Edge. List of outlets on the website

Lanchester Dairies Ltd

Upper House Farm
Lanchester
Co. Durham
DH7 0RL
Tel: 01207 521826
Fax: 01207 521085
Contact: Barry Peacock
Produce: Milk & Cream

Mark Toney

12 Wesley Drive
Benton Square Industrial Estate
Newcastle upon Tyne
NE12 9UP
Tel: 0191 266 1879
Fax: 0191 270 2294
E-Mail: enquiries @marktoney.co.uk

Website: www.marktoney.co.uk
Contact: Anthony and Ann Marcantonio
Produce: Ice creams and Sorbets in all sizes
of tubs, both retail and catering.

Morwick Diary Ice Cream
Morwick Farm
Acklington
Morpeth
Northumberland
NE65 9DG
Tel: 01665 711210
Fax: 01665 711210
E-Mail: howie.morwick@btopenworld.com
Contact: Mrs Howie
Produce: Ice Cream from prize winning
Ayrshire's and Holsteins. 18 flavours. Ice
Cream Parlour also serving coffee and cakes,
open 7 days a week April - October.

Northumberland Cheese Company
Blagdon
Green Lane
Seaton Burn
Northumberland
NE13 6BZ
Tel No: 01670 789798
Fax No: 01670 789644
E-Mail: enquiries@northumberland-
cheese.co.uk
Website: www.northumberland-cheese.co.uk
Contact: Jackie Child
Produce: Hand made small production of
regional specialist artisan cheeses using
vegetarian rennet; Available in cutting
@2kgs; Truckle@500gms or Wedges
@125gms.

Connoisseurs Choice
Cows Milk: Cheviot; Coquetdale; Reiver;
Northumberland X Mature. Jersey Milk:
Chevington; Goats Milk: Brinkburn;
Premium Range: Cows Milk: Hadrian;
Northumberland with Chives, Garlic, Nettle,
Smoked, Northumberland Original; Jersey
Milk: Kielder; Goats Milk: Elsdon Sheep's
Milk: Redesdale.

Northumbrian Pedigree
Marley Cote Walls
Slaley
Hexham
Northumberland
NE47 0DQ
Tel No: 0434 673244
E-Mail: paul@northumbrianpedigree.com
Website: www.northumbrianpedigree.com
Contact: Paul Baynes
Produce: Quality GM Free Milk and Cream
produced from the Marley Cote herd of
Pedigree Dairy Shorthorns and Ayrshire's.
Directly from"Moo to You"

Wheelbirks Dairy Produce
Wheelbirks Farm
Stocksfield
Northumberland
NE43 7HY
Tel No: 01661 842613
Fax No: 01661 842613
E-Mail: enquiries@wheelbirks.co.uk
Website: www.wheelbirks.co.uk
Contact: Tom & Hugh Richardson
Produce: Jersey milk and cream. Jersey
dairy ice cream
Produce can be bought at the farm through
local shops and pubs. Local shows and
events. South Northumberland and Alnwick
Gardens Tree House Restaurant.

Farm Shops
New Barns Farm Shop
New Barns
Warkworth
Morpeth
Northumberland
NE65 0TR
Tel No: 01665 710035
Fax No: 01665 772531
E-Mail: doreen.forsyth@btinternet.com
Contact: Doreen Forsyth
Produce: Meat, fruit pies, cakes, ready-made
meals, soups, sausages, and home cured
bacon.
Meals in coffee shop.

Fish
Swallow Fish Ltd
2 South Street
Seahouses
Northumberland
NE68 7RB
Tel No: 01665 721052/720580
Fax No 01665 721177
E-Mail: wilkin@swallowfish.co.uk
Website: www.swallowfish.co.uk
Contact: Patrick J. Wilkin
Produce: Smoked salmon, cod, haddock,
kippers, crabs, lobsters, prawns and
homemade speciality pates

Lindisfarne Oysters
West House
Ross Farm
Belford
Northumberland
NE70 7EN
Tel No: 01668 213870
Fax No: 01668 219183
E-Mail: enquiries@lindisfarneoysters.co.uk
Website: www.lindisfarneoysters.co.uk
Contact: Christopher & Helen Sutherland
Produce: Pacific Oysters (also known as
Rock or Gigas Oysters) are available for sale
all year round and are carefully reared in the
North Sea, using only natural resources in
the seawater for their food. All oysters are
accompanied with their own health mark to
say that they were purified live bivalve
molluscs, with a dispatch centre approval
number.

Fresh Produce
Carroll's Heritage Potatoes Ltd
Tiptoe Farm
Cornhill-on-Tweed
Northumberland
TD12 4XD
Tel No: 01890 883060
Fax No: 01890 883060
E-Mail: info@heritage-potatoes.co.uk
Website: www.heritage-potatoes.co.uk
Contact: Anthony Carroll
Produce: Growers and suppliers of gourmet
varieties of Heritage Potatoes which offer
unique cooking qualities, special flavour and
taste, interesting colours and shapes, and
give the consumer a taste of history. LEAF
Marque accredited, offering a fully traceable
food production system. The potatoes are
attractively packaged and distributed all over
Britain.

J. Craig's Ltd
Tritlington Hall
Morpeth
Northumberland
NE61 3ED
Tel No: 01670 790223
Fax No: 01670 790520
E-Mail: jcraigsltd@farming.co.uk
Contact: Joanna Craigs
Produce: raspberries, strawberries, winter
vegetables; potatoes, turnips, cabbage,
asparagus & leeks

The Herb Patch
Brockwell House
Newlands
Ebchester
Co. Durham
DH8 9JA
Tel No: 01207 562099
E-Mail: herbs@brockwell01.freeserve.co.uk
Website: www.brockwell01.freeserve.co.uk
Contact: David Potts
Produce: Herb plants, herb mixes, jellies and
stuffing's

North East Organic Growers
Earth Balance
West Sleekburn Farm
Bomarsund
Bedlington
Northumberland
NE22 7AD
Tel No: 01670 821070
Fax No: 01670 821026
E-Mail: neog@care4free.het
Website: www.neog.co.uk
Contact: Alasdair Wilson, Phil Tyler
Produce: organic box scheme, organic
vegetables

Meat, Poultry & Game

Broom House Farm
Witton Gilbert
Durham
Co Durham
DH7 6TR
Tel: 0191 371 9697
Fax: 0191 371 9698
E-Mail: janegray@totalise.co.uk
Website: www.broomhousedurham.co.uk
Produce: Fresh Meat, Homemade Sausages and Frozen meals. Visitors centre, room hire with catering.

Broom Mill Farm
West Auckland
Co. Durham
DL12 9PJ
Tel No: 01388 834564
Fax No: 01388 835299
E-Mail: broommillfarm@aol.com
Website: www.broommillfarm.co.uk
Contact: Matthew & Tracy Betney
Produce: Home bred pork, traditional dry cured bacon, smoked and unsmoked, gammon slices and joints. Homemade speciality pork sausages and seasoned pork

Middle May Lamb
Middle Coldcoats
Ponteland
Newcastle upon Tyne
NE20 0DC
Tel No: 01661 872825
E-Mail: carron@craighead.freeserve.co.uk
Contact: Carron Craighead
Produce: Fresh Spring Lamb: lamb cuts, joints, koftas, chops. Ready made Middle May Moussaka

Moorhouse Farm & Coffee Shop
21 Station Road
Stannington
Morpeth
Northumberland
NE61 6BX
Tel No: 01670 789016
Fax No: 01670 789016
E-Mail: ian@ivypigs.fsnet.co.uk
Contact: Ian and Victoria Byatt
Produce: Fresh pork, beef and lamb from our family farm. Dry cured bacon, gammon sausages, burgers are a few of the products from our large butchery range. The deli offers our own cooked meats, pies and pates. Enjoy local foods including cheese, ice cream, jams, flour, cakes, fresh veg. and much more. Take time in our coffee shop to sample our home cooked produce. Open Tuesday to Sunday, off the A1 at Stannington Station.

Northumbrian Rare Meat
Herding Hill
Shield Hill
Haltwhistle
Northumberland
NE49 9NW
Tel No: 01434 320668
Contact: Debbie Rayson
Produce: Home bred Rare Breed Dexter Cattle, Pigs and Sheep

Northumbrian Quality Meats Ltd
Monkridge Hill Farm
West Woodburn
Northumberland
NE48 2TU
Tel No: 01434 270184
Fax No: 01434 270320
E-Mail: steve@northumbrian-organic-meat.co.uk
Website: www.northumbrian-organic-meat.co.uk
Contact: Steve Ramshaw
Produce: Award winning organic Angus Beef and Blackface Lamb. Rare breed organic Pork. Organic sweet cured Bacon, Gammon & Sausages. Organic Chickens & Eggs. In season, wild Northumbrian Game.

Piperfield Pork
The Dovecote
Lowick
Berwick upon Tweed
TD15 2QE
Tel No: 01289 388543
E-Mail: grahampeterhead@yahoo.com
Contact: Graham Head
Produce: Top quality Middle White pork, sausages, award winning sausages and bacon, Air Dried Chorizo, Glazed Hams.

Teesdale Game and Poultry
82 Galgate
Barnard Castle
County Durham
DL12 8BJ
Tel No: 01833 637153
Fax No: 01833 637153
E-Mail: teesdalegame@aol.com
Website: www.teesdalegame.co.uk
Contact: Stephen and Alison Morrell
Produce: Fresh local Game: Grouse, Pheasant, Mallard, Partridge, Hare, Rabbit and Woodpigeon. All cuts of Venison, Venison Sausages, Venison Mince, Homemade Game pies, and Smoked products

Well Hung and Tender
Baldersbury Hill Farm
Berwick upon Tweed
Northumberland
TD15 1UY
Tel No: 01289 386216
E-Mail: info@wellhungandtender.com
Contact: Donald & Sarah MacPherson
Produce: Prime Aberdeen Angus beef produced on the farm. All naturally reared and grass fed. Hung 'on the bone' for a minimum of 3 weeks. Normally pre-packed and can be cut to customers' requirements, fresh and frozen.

Preserves, Honey, Dressings, Pickles and Sauces

Chain Bridge Honey Farm
Horncliffe
Berwick upon Tweed
Northumberland
Tel No: 01289 386362
E-Mail: info@chainbridgehoney.co.uk
Website: www.chainbridgehoney.co.uk
Contact: Willie Robson
Produce: Pure honey products and by-products
Tweedside honey, clear, heather, aromatic and clover, honey mustards, pure beeswax candles and polish
Cosmetics: creams, ointments and soaps. Visitors centre.

James Ross & Son (Newcastle) Ltd
The Preserving Works
Newburn
Newcastle upon Tyne
NE15 9TU
Tel No: 0191 267 6321
Fax: 0191 264 0832
E-Mail: chris.pennison@jamesross.co.uk
Website: www.pickles-r-ross.co.uk
Contact: Chris Pennison
Produce: Pickled products - gourmet range, core range, retail, wholesale and catering packs.

Mason & Graham
470 Old Durham Road
Low Fell
Gateshead
Tyne & Wear
NE9 5DR
Tel No: 0191 4915341
E-Mail: masonandgraham@blueyonder.co.uk
Contact: Mirella Graham
Produce: Oils, Dressings, Nuts & Savoury Jellies

Maysan Ltd

Meadowfield Industrial Estate
Ponteland
Newcastle upon Tyne
NE20 9SD
Tel No: 01661 823055
Fax: 01661 824506
E-Mail: maysanfoods@eurotel
broadband.com
Contact: Denise Harrison
Produce: Chinese Curry Pastes and Powders

Pickled Pink

Fantastic Indian pickles and chutney. Superb
traditionally English pickles and probably the
best lemon curd you will ever taste. Try our
delicious Mediterranean anti-pastas and our
unique Chili Sauce . See you at the next
Farmers Market !
Website:www.pickledpink.co.uk

Wildon Grange

Romaldkirk
Barnard Castle
Co Durham
DL12 9EW
Tel No: 01833 650587
E-Mail: dot@wildongrange.co.uk
Website: www.wildongrange.co.uk
Contact: Dorothy Ritzema
Produce: Salad Dressings and Relishes.

Wynbeech

Absolute Gourmet
Vallum Farm
Military Road
East Wall Houses
Northumberland
NE18 0LL
Tel No: 01434 672006
Fax No: 01434 672006
E-Mail: wynbeech@btinternet.com
Website: www.wynbeech.co.uk
Contact: David Appleby or Jayne Appleby
Produce: Superior Quality Preserves,
Marmalades, Curds, Chutney's, Relishes,
Sauces, Flavoured Mustards, Herb & Spice
Flavoured Oils & Vinegars, and Herbal &
Spiced Hand Creams, using their own
produce or produce that is locally sourced.
Traditional & Gourmet ranges all made with
no artificial additives.

Ready Meals

Fresh Element

The Kitchens
John Buddle Work Village
Buddle Road
Newcastle upon Tyne
NE4 8AW
Tel No: 0191 226 7323
Fax No: 0191 226 7327
E-Mail: pete@freshelement.co.uk
         andy@freshelement.co.uk
Website: www.freshelement.co.uk
Contact: Pete Hunt, Andy Ross
Produce: High Quality meals using fresh,
natural and local ingredients. Range also
includes Soups, Pates and Terrines. Retail
Outlets: Country Whey, Jesmond. Rehills,
Jesmond. Out of This World, Gosforth.
Deli@Darras, Darras Hall. Dobbies Farm
Shop, Ponteland. The Food Shop, Durham.
Café Chill, The Sage, Great Park. Farmers'
Markets attended: Newcastle, Hexham,
Tynemouth, Morpeth, Berwick, Alnwick, and
Durham.

Harvest Foods

Whinfield Drive
Aycliffe Industrial Park
Newton Aycliffe
Co Durham
DL5 6AU
Tel No: 01325 319039
Fax No: 01325 315813
E-Mail: info@harvestfoods.co.uk
Website: www.harvestfoods.co.uk
Contact: Colin Whitham
Produce: Frozen Ready Meals Manufacturer.

Mr BBQ Ltd

37 Glebe Mews
Bedlington
Northumberland
NE22 6LJ
Tel No: 0845 226 9363
Fax No: 0845 226 9363
E-Mail: Linda@mr-bbq.co.uk
Website: www.mr-bbq.co.uk
Contact: Linda Bradley
Produce: Barbecue beans.

Tanfield Food Company Ltd

Hownsgill Park
Consett
Co. Durham
DH8 7NY
Tel No: 01207 588 783
Fax No: 01207 582 915
Email: kim@tanfieldfood.com
Website: www.tanfieldfood.com
Contact: Kim McKie
Produce: Producers of the brand 'Look What
We Found'. A superb range of gourmet
meals, made in small batches, with regional
ingredients. The unique use of steam
pressure cooking allows longer shelf-life and
ambient distribution.

Redemption Food Company Ltd

Unit 5A
Number One Industrial Estate
Consett
Co Durham
DH8 6SR
Tel: 01207 508 111 or Ian Blair 07834 652999
Fax: 01207 508 999
E-mail: ian@redemptionfood.co.uk
Contact: Office - Christine Morrison or Sales
Director Ian Blair
Produce: The Redemption Food Company
has been formed specifically to produce
Fresh Soups and Sauces for the growing
food service market. We will supply - the very
best products made with only the very best
ingredients. Innovation, competitive pricing,
market support and service.

Weardale Soup

Christine Peart Elm Cottage, Westgate,
Bishop Auckland DL13 1LP. Home-made
gluten-free vegetarian organic soups made
using regional vegetables, cream & butter. All
soups are free from thickeners, stabilizers
and preservatives.Available as 1/2 litre to 5
litre pails. Beetroot & parsnip; Weardale
Vegetable; Carrot with Cumin & Caraway;
Cream of Asparagus; Spinach, Pea & Herb;
Tomato & Road Pepper; Cream of Leek,
Onion & Potato Available from Barnard Castle
Farmers Market; Burtree House Farm Shop;
Alsop & Hedleys, Indoor Market, Durham;
Donaldsons, Stanhope; Organiks, Hexham;
Wolsingham Paper Shop (The Butler's
Pantry); Harperley P.O.W.Farm Shop; Direct (
telephone first)
Tel: 01388 517384
Mob: 07855 044970
Email: christine@weardaleorganicsoup.co.uk

Many thanks to Northumbria Larder for their
assistance in compiling this section. For
further information on quality produce from
the North East visit:
www.northumbria-larder.co.uk

CONTRIBUTORS

AGE BAR & KITCHEN
72 Claypath, Durham, DH1 1QT
Tel: 0191 375 7750, www.agebarandkitchen.co.uk

BALTIC
The Rooftop Restaurant, South Shore Road, Gateshead
Tel: 0191 440 4949

BARN MOVING ON!
The Biscuit Factory, Shieldfield, Newcastle
Tel: 0191 230 3338

BLACK DOOR RESTAURANT
32 Clayton Street West, Newcastle, NE1 5DZ
Tel: 0191 261 6295

BLACKFRIARS RESTAURANT
Friars Street, Newcastle, NE1 4XN
Tel: 0191 261 5945 www.blackfriarsrestaurant.co.uk

CAFÉ LOWREY
33-35 The Broadway, Darras Hall, Ponteland, NE20 9PW
Tel: 01661 820357, www.cafelowrey.co.uk

CLOSE HOUSE COUNTRY CLUB
Close House, Heddon-on-the-Wall, Newcastle, NE15 0HT
Tel: 01661 852255 www.closehouse.co.uk

CRAB & LOBSTER
Dishforth Road, Asenby, near Thirsk, YO7 3QL
Tel: 01845 577286 www.crabandlobster.co.uk

CRATHORNE HALL
Crathorne, Yarm, North Yorkshire, TS15 0AR
Tel: 01642 700398 www.handpicked.co.uk

THE FEVERSHAM ARMS HOTEL
Helmsley, North Yorkshire, YO62 5AG
Tel : 01439 770766 www.fevershamarmshotel.com

FISHERMAN'S LODGE
Deep Dene House, Jesmond Dene, Newcastle, NE7 7BQ
Tel: 0191 281 3281 www.tomscompanies.com

GISBOROUGH HALL
Whitby Lane, Guisborough, North Yorkshire, TS14 6PT
Tel: 0870 400 8191 www.gisborough-hall.co.uk

GREENS
13 Bridge Street, Whitby, North Yorkshire YO22 4BG
Tel: 01947 600284 www.greensofwhitby.com

LA RIVIERA
Pipewellgate, Swing Bridge, Gateshead, NE8 2BJ
Tel: 0191 477 7070 www.lariviera.co.uk

LONGHIRST HALL
Longhirst, Morpeth, Northumberland, NE61 3LL
Tel: 01670 791348 www.longhirst.co.uk

MANDALAY
1-2 Holly Avenue West, Jesmond, Newcastle
Tel: 0191 281 8281 www.themandalay.co.uk

MATFEN HALL
Matfen, Northumberland, NE20 0RH
Tel: 01661 886500 www.matfenhall.com

MCCOY'S AT THE TONTINE
The Cleveland Tontine, Northallerton, North Yorkshire, DL6 3JD
Tel: 01609 882671 www.mccoysatthetontine.co.uk

CONTRIBUTORS

OLDFIELDS RESTAURANT

9 Osbourne Road, Jesmond, Newcastle, NE2 2AE

Tel: 0191 212 1210 www.oldfieldsrestaurants.com

PARADISO

1 Market Lane, Newcastle, NE1 6QQ

Tel: 0191 221 1240 www.gustouk.co.uk

PRICKLY PEAR

4 Esplanade Mews, Sunderland, SR2 7BQ

Tel: 0191 564 0982

PUMPHOUSE

Farm Road, Houghall, Durham, DH1 3PJ

Tel: 0191 386 9189 www.thepumphouserestaurant.co.uk

RAFFLES

The Croft, Croft on Tees, Darlington, DL2 2ST

Tel: 01325 720319, www.rafflesuk.com

ROUÉ DINING ROOM AND LOUNGE

Gilesgate House, 4-6 Gilesgate, Hexham,

Northumberland, NE46 3NJ

Tel: 01434 602110

THE STABLES

The Granary, Wynyard Village, TS22 5QQ

Tel: 01740 644074

SEAHAM HALL & THE SERENITY SPA

Lord Byrons Walk, Seaham, County Durham, SR7 7AD

Tel: 0191 516 1400 www.tomscompanies.com

SECCO RISTORANTE SALENTINO

86, Pilgrim St, Newcastle, NE1 6SG

Tel: 0191 230 0444 www.seccouk.com

SIDNEY'S RESTAURANT

3-5 Percy Park Road, Tynemouth, North Shields, NE30 4LZ

Tel: 0191 257 8500 www.sidneys.co.uk

THE SMITHS ARMS

Carlton Village, Stockton-On-Tees, TS21 1EA

Tel: 01740 630471 www.thesmithscarlton.co.uk

THE STAR INN

Harome, York, YO62 5JE

Tel: 01439 770397 www.thestaratharome.co.uk

THE TREEHOUSE

The Alnwick Garden, Denwick Lane,

Alnwick, Northumberland, NE66 1YU

Tel: 01665 511852 www.alnwickgarden.com

VUJON

29 Queen Street, Quayside, Newcastle, NE1 3UG

Tel: 0191 221 0601 www.vujon.com